THE HOUSE BETWEEN
EARTH AND SKY

Harvesting New American Folktales

JOSEPH DANIEL SOBOL

Teacher Ideas Press
Portsmouth, NH

Teacher Ideas Press
A division of Reed Elsevier Inc.
361 Hanover Street
Portsmouth, NH 03801-3912
www.teacherideaspress.com

Offices and agents throughout the world

A percentage of the royalties from this book is being donated to the Neighborhood Arts Program of the Chicago Department of Cultural Affairs and to the Chicago Board of Education for their sponsorship and hosting of the Chicago TESOL Folklore Project.

Library of Congress Cataloging-in-Publication Data
Sobol, Joseph Daniel.
    The house between earth and sky: harvesting new American folktales / by Joseph Daniel Sobol.
        p. cm.
    Includes bibliographical references.
    ISBN 1-59158-080-3 (alk. paper)
    1. Folklore—United States. 2. Oral tradition—United States. 3. Storytelling—United States.   I. Title.
    GR105.S56 2005
    398'.0973—dc22   2004020326

Editor: Suzanne Barchers
Production Coordinator: Angela Rice
Typesetter: Westchester Book Services
Cover design: Gaile Ivaska
Manufacturing: Steve Bernier

Printed in the United States of America on acid-free paper

09   08   07   06   05   ML   1   2   3   4   5

CONTENTS

ACKNOWLEDGMENTS

First, this book would not exist without the patience, support, and inspiration of my wife, Mitzi Chambers Sobol. Her tales from the front lines of the urban educational battlefield gave me the initial idea for the residencies that became the Chicago TESOL Folklore Project. Next, the Chicago Department of Cultural Affairs Neighborhood Arts Program gave the financial support for that first residency at Roosevelt High School and also for subsequent residencies at Senn and Mather High Schools. An additional residency at Pierce International Middle School was supported by Scrap Mettle/Soul, a project of Community Performance, Inc., with the help of the Chicago Community Trust.

The principals, ESL coordinators, and ESL teachers at the schools were essential partners in each of the residencies. I would especially like to thank Roosevelt's principal at the time, Mr. Rafael Sanchez, Roosevelt's ESL Coordinator, Margo Ventrelli, and ESL teachers Bridget Galligan, Jocelyn Hass, Carol Tully, and Kim Unterberger; Pierce principal Janice M. Rosales and TESOL specialist Kathy Myers; Senn principal Judy Hernandez, ESL coordinator Kathryn Khoshaba, ESL teachers Drue Hoffman and Theresa Pratt, and art teacher Barbara Singer, whose lunchtime hospitality was a boon; Mather principal John Butterfield, assistant principal Betty Martinez, TESOL specialists Darlene Defina, Natasha Oussenko, Karen Meyer, Diane Munoz, and Georgette Rohde, drama teacher Lois Weiss, and computer specialist Pat McArdle.

To the good folks at Libraries Unlimited/Heinemann, I owe special gratitude for their cheerful and efficient partnership on this book. Suzanne Barchers, Angie Rice, Karyn Slutsky, and their team have been supportive and patient beyond measure.

I especially thank the students and their family members who gave their stories, proverbs, beliefs, remedies, recipes, reminiscences, and their good will to this project. You have the wisdom of the world within you. Now, thanks to you, some sparks of that wisdom are set here for the world to behold.

INTRODUCTION

The Education Tree

There are twelve third-year and transitional English as a Second-Language (ESL) classes at Roosevelt High School, in the Albany Park community on Chicago's Northwest Side. These twelve classes contain about 250 immigrant students from over thirty nations and language groups. Just over a generation ago this was a largely Jewish neighborhood, and Roosevelt was a mostly middle-class and academically accelerated school. Now it is a little United Nations. Roughly half the school's population is foreign born, and three-quarters speak a language besides English in the home. Walk down any hall and you will hear Spanish, Arabic, Urdu, Gujarati, Malayalam, Punjabi, Tagalog, Serbo-Croatian, Romanian, Albanian, Somali, Cambodian, or Vietnamese. It is a vast confusion of tongues, and yet there is something inspiring about it too: the forest loam of a new America, based on an immigrant dream as old as Brendan the Navigator.

On November 13, 1995, at twenty after seven in the morning, I found myself facing two of those classes—fifty or so students in various stages of wakening. It was the culmination of over a year of planning, grant writing, hope, disappointment, rekindled hope, and furious, last-minute preparation—a typical schedule for a laborer in the fields of public arts grant programs in an era of budgetary drought. But now, finally, a folkloric and educational hunch would be put to the test.

When I first caught the storytelling and folklore bugs in the early eighties, I did what many had done before me—I moved to North Carolina, where, presumably, "real" folklore could still be found. And in fact I did find a continuity with the past there and a closeness to the land that keeps old ways vividly present and breeds good traditional storytelling. When I moved to Chicago at the end of that decade, the question nagged me: Where could that continuity and closeness be found in an urban environment?

The obvious answer was: in the immigrant communities, which were constantly replenishing themselves from older worlds. But with a very few exceptions like the Irish, Scottish, Cornish, or Appalachian (in effect an immigrant group within these United States), the immigrant communities were fenced off from me by the primal barrier of language as well as by other barriers—geography, occupation, socioeconomic class, and so forth—of urban life. There are places where these barriers can be bridged, relationships developed, and guides and interpreters found—community centers, churches, work sites, and, of course, certain taverns. But one institution has traditionally brought a variety of people together with the explicit intention of guiding their transitions—from child to adult, from unlettered to literate, from stranger to citizen—and that is the schools. High school bilingual and ESL* programs could be seen as basic training programs for cultural interpreters, and if only the initial red tape could be negotiated, nowhere would I, as a folklorist, have a more natural role in the process. ESL/TESOL students live in two worlds at once. Most come from cultures that are fundamentally oral and deeply traditional, yet they are now immersed in a world where oral traditions are fast being pushed aside. I hoped that this project would give them a medium for exploring and savoring their wondrous and perilous transitions. Learning and sharing multicultural folktales, conducting interviews, transcribing and translating stories—these are exercises with great value. They provide a way for students to discover some of the potency of what they specially bring to the carnival of American culture. They give students a chance to meet their elders on a plane where the elders are at a cultural advantage, rather than a disadvantage, and so they promote pride and respect between stressed generations. They can even provide an antidote, if momentarily, to the tide of defensive obliviousness that sweeps immigrants' children toward an homogenized identity as "Americans," leaving their heritage as something to be teased out by their own wistful grandchildren, only after so much has already been lost.

But beyond this, I hoped for an end product, a book of stories from the residency. I knew that a book of the students' stories would be a concrete expression of school pride in students' cultural richness and diversity, and so it was written into the design of the grant proposal. I had no special reason to think that the stories uncovered by this random group of ESL students would be of sufficient interest to stand by themselves for a wider reading public, but I could always hope, wonder, and do what any fisherman does—cast the net and wait.

For the rest of that November day, and then intensively over a three-month period, I worked with ten of the twelve ESL classes at Roosevelt High School. I began by telling Jack tales, long wonder tales from Appalachian oral tradition, because I know them well, because I wanted the students to hear what oral traditions sound like in English, and because among the tales of a boy named Jack there are fool stories, trickster stories, and hero stories that have parallel versions from all over the world. I kept reminding the students that these folktales were not just mine, but a common inheritance of many peoples.

Some students looked at me with carefully cultivated indifference, but scattered among those looks were sparks of recognition. Several of the Bosnian students nodded as if they knew just what

---

*The terms ESL and TESOL—Teaching English for Speakers of Other Languages—are incremental attempts to capture the complexity of the language situation in American public schools. The classes I taught at Roosevelt High School in 1995–1996 were called ESL, but by the time I was teaching at Mather High School in 2000, the same classes were called TESOL. The terms will be used more or less interchangeably in this book, though TESOL seems to be gaining ascendance.

I was talking about. Rahama from Somalia said, "We have many stories like that in my family. But I can't say them in English." During fourth period, a Palestinian boy named David said, "We heard stories like that from my grandmother." And during seventh period, two of David's sisters, Amal and Nahil, got started telling some of those stories and clearly could have kept going for days. The discovery process was underway.

In the second week we began a workshop on folklore collecting. We started with simple genres, such as proverbs and beliefs, and moved on to rhymes, remedies, recipes, and, finally, folktales. The students were trained in the process of conducting folklore interviews. They were given lists of open-ended questions to ask and likely types of folkloric expression to search for in their families and neighborhoods. They were shown how to use cassette recorders to tape interviews, how to transcribe tapes, and how to write down stories from memory and notes. The interviews were done in their native languages and afterwards translated into English. Their ESL teachers and I then collected their interviews and translations. The students received a grade and I received the raw materials to edit and arrange into a booklet of folklore from Roosevelt High School—new American folktales from inner-city Chicago.

The results quickly surpassed my early hopes. I remember the thrill when I first went to study folklore in North Carolina of knowing that I had come to a fountainhead of venerable oral traditions. It may seem strange but the feeling I had while reading my ESL students' assignments was quite similar. But these students have carried into the aging halls of a Chicago high school traditions from every corner of the world, and these traditions draw deeply from what ancient writers called the "Ocean of Story."

Glinting from the rough manuscripts were tales that I recognized from countless collections of the best in traditional storytelling—always changed and renewed through the process of migrating and settling in new places, new times, new tongues. These were the gemstones of oral tradition— the stories that keep their crystalline forms despite every metamorphosis of language, culture, and generation. There were classic wonder tales and chilling tales of supernatural beings. There were tales from widely known folktale cycles about tricksters like Nasruddin (Hodja in Bosnia and Turkey, Gioha in Syria and Yemen), Somalia's Egal Shidaad, and the Indian jester Gopal and about fools like the Mexican or Philippine Lazy Juan and the Puerto Rican Juan Bobo. There were animal tales from Asia and India, much like those found in the world's oldest Sanskrit story collections, and everywhere there were wry fables of hard-earned wisdom.

I took the rough translations and selected, edited, and retold them for English language readers in a booklet that was then inexpensively printed and bound for the students and faculty at Roosevelt. I was careful to keep the original plots, sequences, and, wherever possible, the original language of the students' work. I gave preference to stories that bore the marks of immediate family and community oral traditions and left out many fine stories that were clearly derived from printed sources. It was a process like polishing and setting gemstones so that their qualities can catch the light. Those stories that had already been polished by print needed no further labor from us.

The success of that first Chicago ESL Folklore Project led to several more grant-supported residencies between 1996 and 2000. Each of the schools in which I worked had its own astonishing blend of cultures, languages, and folkways, drawn from the character of its neighborhood. Each residency culminated in the compilation of a booklet that was left with the students and with the school. And each of those collections comprised a small sampling of potential new American traditions, caught in the precise moment of transition from Old World to New.

There are dozens more high schools in Chicago and its suburbs with immigrant mixes at least as rich, and I could have gladly busied myself with these projects endlessly if other work had not led me away from the area in 2000. But I now consider the hunch confirmed and the method well proven and applicable to any area with strong second-language communities—which increasingly means nearly every town of any size in the United States, Canada, Britain, or, for that matter, anywhere in the industrialized world. It is ready to present both as process and product, and to be transferred to other communities, other hands.

Hence the design of this book: When you have finished, you will have experienced a secondary ESL folklore residency step by step, week by week. Each step will be explained and illustrated, and in each chapter you will find representative selections of the kinds of materials that in similar projects you would be both presenting to and collecting from students and their local communities. Among the materials and assignments, though, you will also find scattered nuggets of personal experience, reflections and ideas about the process, and, of course, stories. The book culminates in a selection of international folktales from the four Chicago ESL residencies, arranged geographically—the world as encountered in a handful of neighborhoods.

Toward the end of my first residency at Roosevelt High School, a pair of cousins from Pakistan, Ahmed Syed and Yoosufani Mujeebullah, shared the following story, "The Education Tree."

> Long ago in Pakistan there was a king who had a counselor, a very educated man. But to make more of himself in the eyes of the king, this counselor made up a tale. He said that he had heard there was a tree in India that, if you ate its fruit, you would never grow old or die.
>
> The king said, "But this is astonishing! I must have this fruit! If you know where it is, you must go and find it and bring it to me!"
>
> The wise man couldn't admit to the king that he had made the story up. So he packed his things and went to India, hoping that perhaps he could in fact find such a fruit.
>
> He searched for it in every city and every town and village over the length and breadth of India. But, of course, he never found the fruit. And after several years he thought that he would go home and live out his days in obscurity.
>
> Just before he reached the border of Pakistan, he saw an old, old man coming toward him who looked as if he had all the world's wisdom graven on his face. If any man could tell me about such a fruit from such a tree, he thought, it's this man. So he thought he would try to put the question one more time.
>
> The old man smiled when he heard it. "The tree you are looking for is called the Education Tree," he said. "Some call it a tree, some call it a river, some call it an ocean, some call it the world. If you truly eat the fruit of that tree, your mind will always be nimble, your heart will be young, and your thoughts will be immortal, because they will be the great thoughts that live on with the wise forever."
>
> The minister thanked the old man and left India. He went to the king, and with a contrite heart he told the truth of his journey and what he had learned. And the king rewarded him well.

The original Latin root of the word "education," *educare,* means "to lead out from within." In that sense this project represents a model of what creative multicultural education can be. To bring the new multicultural nation into being it is insufficient either to spoon-feed European traditions and values to new arrivals or to present them with a prepackaged vision of world cultures. It is essential to ask the students themselves to dig at the roots of their own traditions, to pick and choose and to bring the harvest into relationship with those of their fellow students and of their teachers. Then they may discover for themselves that there is a genuine and fruitful relationship, a budding sense of cultural harmony, a new song composed out of many old themes but that has never been sounded in quite this way before.

Most traditional stories concern themselves directly with education—not in the modern sense of accumulating facts and techniques, but in the traditional sense of learning to distinguish right from wrong, just from unjust, wise from foolish, true from false, good from evil. Traditional stories, along with their cultural matrix of proverbs, beliefs, songs, festivals, rituals, and family and community relationships, *are* the educational systems of oral cultures. They are the seeds that, sown in the soul and properly tended, can grow into the Education Tree: the cultivated self. As we have seen so harshly dramatized these past few years, it grows ever more urgent, for the sake of peace and world survival, that these new plants be carefully tended and these new songs be sung.

PART 1

THE RIVERS OF FOLKLORE

According to statistics compiled by the nonprofit Center for Immigration Studies, more than 1.2 million legal and illegal immigrants combined now settle in the United States each year. "The number of immigrants living in the United States has more than tripled since 1970, from 9.6 million to 28.4 million. By historical standards, the number of immigrants living in the United States is unprecedented. Even at the peak of the great wave of early twentieth-century immigration, the number of immigrants living in the United States was of less than half what it is today. The 11.2 million immigrants who indicated they arrived between 1990 and 2000 plus the 6.4 million children born to immigrants in the United States during the 1990s are equal to almost 70 percent of U.S. population growth over the last ten years. Immigration accounts for virtually all of the national increase in public school enrollment over the last two decades. In 2000, there were 8.6 million school-age children from immigrant families in the United States." (http://www.cis.org/articles/2001/back 101.html)

The pressure of immigrants pouring into America's public schools is a fact of contemporary life that drives, for good and ill, many of the changes in our educational field. This river of new arrivals is made up of many streams of culture. Out of Latin America, the Caribbean, Eastern Europe, the Middle East, Africa, and Asia, these streams join at the gates of our inner-city schools. How we respond—whether with welcome or denial, accommodation or resistance, open-hearted questions or closed-minded answers—will determine a great deal about the society we create in this century. What follows is one set of tools for preparing an informed welcome. Folklore and storytelling carry the forms of a common language, one that transcends the simple divisions of "ours" and "theirs." It can help set a table at which all are invited to serve and to eat.

1. WEEK ONE: TO BEGIN

Welcome to Pierce International School, a K–8 school in the Edgewater neighborhood of Chicago's North Side. It's a stout, handsome, three-story stone edifice from the distant heyday of Chicago city school construction. Its phenomenal overcrowding will presumably be relieved by the brand-new building going up in the former playground next door. Meanwhile, there are classes meeting in the halls, food carts standing in the lobby, and files stacked in boxes that shuttle from one set of temporary offices to the next. The faces that swarm past make up the typical urban American rainbow—from sub-Saharan black to Nordic pink and every shade in between—but the accent is heavily on the desert earth tones of Mexico.

I am here for four weeks, collecting folktales, legends, imaginative fictions, and personal stories from a group of sixth-to-eighth-grade TESOL students. The school has incorporated my residency in its after-school enrichment program. So this group of students, at least to some extent, should be volunteers.

And so it is. The group that straggles in on my first day in the classroom turns out to consist of twenty Mexican students, ages eleven to fourteen. There are many other nationalities, languages, and culture groups represented at this international school, but without large enough peer blocs to shelter them against the ever-present terror of difference, none of the Asian, Caribbean, African, East European, or South American students have dared to join. So

what we have here is a Mexican-American folklore club—even more narrowly, the folklore of a wide triangular slice of Mexico that has the capital city at its apex and the Pacific states of Michoacan and Oaxaca at either end.

For four weeks, four afternoons a week, I tell the group stories, share information about folktales, legends, and other forms of international folklore, and prompt the students with questions to ponder and to take home to their families and communities. A couple of students catch on immediately and come right back at me with stories, proverbs, and beliefs. Most stonewall, giggling, whispering, or shaking their heads in denial with the pursed half-smiles of preteen Mona Lisas. By the end of the four weeks, however, we are building a nice representative folklore collection and there's a sweet feeling of fellowship in the room. Word gets out that the last day of the residency is my birthday, and the class has a surprise cake waiting for me that day, with my name in blue frosting and my age in flaming red letters. We eat, drink, and make merry. But the tales and proverbs that we collected are the real meal.

We collected them as written by the students both in English and in Spanish. Then Mrs. Kathy Myers, the TESOL specialist, and I entered the texts into the word processor. I took the liberty of adding some connective material to the English versions. These students bring a great deal of nourishment to the American cultural feast. They have a tremendous amount to teach us if we are only willing to learn, and if we can help them learn to teach.

So how do we begin?

Educated and Uneducated: The Discipline of Folklore and the Folk Art of Storytelling

The tools we will be wielding in this project are the ancient traditional folk art of storytelling and the relatively modern scholarly discipline of folklore. So it would be helpful to know a bit about these two overlapping patches in the quilt of human heritage.

It is difficult for most of us now even to imagine an environment that is not saturated with written and electronic media to transmit and store information. But it is important to try to imagine such an environment, if only to put ourselves in the shoes of many of those students who enter our TESOL classrooms. In such an environment, storytelling sits at the center of cultural experience. Spoken language is the first technology devised by humans for representing ourselves, and the breadth and variety of stories preserved in oral cultures is simply astonishing to anyone accustomed to getting their stories from print. But when storytelling was the primary technology for transmitting cultural knowledge, virtually all important community understandings in the realms of human relations, spiritual laws, or occupational lore could be—indeed, had to be—indexed in stories. The catalog of ships from Homer's *Iliad,* which scholars now concede originated as oral poetry, is a famous example of an oral traditional encyclopedia—the entire realm of Achaean maritime crafts collected within the compass of a storytelling set piece.

Storytelling has been practiced over the ages by people from every land and every walk of life. Some practitioners would have been hereditary specialists with high status in their tribes or communities. The chief tradition bearers of intact oral cultures—whether known as bards, griots, *ashoks, guslars, biwa-roshis,* seanachies, and so forth—were trained artists of a high order, carrying repertoires of epic songs, wonder tales, legends, and teaching stories that could stretch for hundreds of hours on end. Other traditional storytellers would have been quite ordinary in outward station, distinguished from their neighbors only by a particular aptitude for a tale or a song. Naturally there would also be much traditional lore that was not specialized, but that would be shared among members of any given culture and would constitute their common inheritance as a group.

Though we still can find them, sometimes unheralded outside of their neighborhoods, sometimes widely recognized as performers and teachers, these dedicated carriers of the bulk of their oral traditions are relatively rare now that print and electronic media have come to dominate so much of the globe. But traditional arts have a life force and an endurance of their own, and they persist in surprising ways in ordinary peoples' lives. Even if there is no unmistakable master storyteller, musician, healer, or craftsperson in an immigrant community, much of the knowledge that would have made one can still be found in dilute form spread across the community as a whole. Although we would certainly welcome the discovery of a master folk artist or two in our school communities, it is mainly this general folk knowledge that we are prospecting for in our TESOL folklore projects.

The scholarly discipline of folklore developed to study these group traditions, to record what could be preserved in writing and in newer media, even as the oral traditions it focused on were rapidly losing their sway. It is poignant to note that the work of folklorists can be seen in various lights in relation to the overthrow of oral traditions by literacy: as symptom, as response, as witting or unwitting agency—or as all of these. Folklore emerged at a critical stage in the transformation of culture from orality to literacy. Thus it is a discipline haunted throughout its history by a sense that the things it seeks to preserve are doomed to obsolescence by the media through which it seeks to preserve them.

The word "folklore" was coined in 1843 by the Englishman William Thoms, based on the term that came to the fore in German Romanticism, *"Volkskunde."* Already by then, Wilhelm and Jacob Grimm had made the collecting of traditional oral stories a core activity of European nationalism. They were followed by scholars in every country in Europe and eventually in the United States. The American Folklore Society was founded in 1888. It was dominated for a long while by scholars of Native American and African American cultures, which were seen as enclaves of unbroken oral tradition within the larger society. Gradually that emphasis has broadened to include many different ethnic cultures within the United States and in their original homelands.

The literary or anthropological biases of earlier folklorists have also evolved and blended into a disciplinary eye that seeks out group-specific expressive practices across a wide spectrum of cultural life. These can include storytelling, music making, folk medicine, cooking, traditional religion and folk beliefs, occupational and recreational crafts, clothing and body adornment, dance and other forms of patterned movement, community celebrations, festivals, rituals, and whatever else may spring from the well of communal expression. In the past few decades, as "pure" oral cultures become ever rarer, folklorists have been focusing on what are called *residual oral traditions,* those (like urban legends and musical subcultures) that arise and flourish in traditional ways, right in the midst of modern community and social life.

In periods of history when literacy makes its first inroads among oral traditional peoples, the works that tend to be written down first are those great works of oral tradition, the epics and the traditional hero tale cycles. These form the foundations of new national cultures. The Hebrew Five Books of Moses, the *Iliad* and *Odyssey* of Homer, the Cuchulain and Finn McCumhal cycles in Ireland, the Finnish Kalevala, the Arthurian legends in England and France, the Decameron in Italy, the Arabian Nights in the Middle East—all of these are collections of tales that would have once been performed orally in a variety of fragmentary pieces and settings. Without writing, of course, stories have no existence independent of their performances. It was the technology of writing that made it possible to knit the tales into new forms of unity—books—and as such to stand for and to bring together scattered tribes of people into national identities—just as it is the electronic media (radio, television, film, and Internet) that are rapidly erasing national boundaries to form the embattled outlines of a global civilization.

This is a process that could and did take many hundreds of years and many stages to develop fully. In earlier stages, literacy would be a craft practiced only by elites. Outside of those exclusive classes, the vast majority of people in agricultural, pastoral, or early industrialized societies would be nonliterate—or literate in only a limited sense—and rely on oral traditions for their primary orientation to the world. In temples of literacy such as the public schools, we are accustomed to thinking of nonliteracy as the most dreadful of blights, and we devote the bulk of our energy toward eradicating it. What we often forget is that nonliteracy is only a blight when it is out of phase with another dominant cultural reality. In a world that expresses itself mainly through alphabetic symbols in visual space, nonliteracy is reasonably defined as a lack of the basic ability to make sense of that environment. In societies where literacy and nonliteracy form the basis of vast power differentials, literacy is a tool of emancipation. But in its own sphere, oral culture is not merely an absence of something essential, but a vivid, integral reality of distinctive richness and depth. It retains that magnetism for those reared within it, even in the face of an altered and suddenly dominant cultural mind-set.

We denigrate that traditional reality at our own peril. The continual outbreaks of folk revivalism over many centuries in Europe and America have been recurrent mass testimonies to this effect: There is something essential in oral traditions that we often leave behind when moving into the brave new worlds defined by print. We might sum up that endangered essence with the words "connectedness" and "community." Print, and now the Internet all the more, unite people in the abstract, within their separated individual spheres, each alone even when sharing a physical space. The spoken word unites people in living, breathing, and organic moments of communal identification. When we turn our backs on this deepest of human needs, we can find it sneaking up behind us in malevolent forms—our own exiled shadows come to haunt us.

At the same time, the complex and volatile layering of our contemporary media environment makes it possible for us now to see orality in a fresh light: not merely as a former world doomed to discredit by the dominant media that have succeeded it, but as a layer of cultural expression that remains powerfully latent within all of us, and that is more or less vividly awakened in different groups and settings. For many of us, the time of greatest potential sensitivity to our oral natures is childhood. This is why storytelling remains a tremendous if often neglected resource in the schools.

In the 1970s, the art of storytelling began to undergo a revival of its own in the United States and other developed countries. The founding in 1973 in Jonesborough, Tennessee, of the first festival devoted entirely to storytelling has heralded a groundswell of interest in the contemporary potentials and uses of the traditional art. It has also spawned a proliferation of professional activity in the field. Artists, educators, librarians, ministers, businesspersons, health care workers, and others have edged away from previous affiliations to declare themselves as storytellers. In so doing, they have created a widening sense of the value and utility of storytelling, both as a performing art in its own right and as a tool in bringing greater depth of understanding to their former occupations.

This same period saw the spread of what came to be known as public folklore—folklorists who were employed not just in scholarly settings to teach and write for other scholars, but also in public programs sponsored by state and local arts and cultural agencies to increase local appreciation of ethnic and regional traditions. Since the founding of the National Endowment for the Arts in 1964, public folklore programs have been seeded in nearly every state in the United States. As I was coming to vocational maturity in the 1980s, it was within this context of the simultaneous burgeoning of professional storytelling and public folklore. It was in order to understand the traditions of storytelling, not simply in the idealized images of the revival movement, but in its actual relationship to surviving traditional communities, that I took up the study of folklore. Together, the folk art and the scholarly discipline provide a powerful set of tools for working with TESOL students in the schools of today's inner cities.

Creating a Team

If you are a professional storyteller or folklorist and you wish to initiate a TESOL folklore residency, it is important to choose a target service area and to research the TESOL populations of the neighborhoods and schools within it. Most school district offices have this information in the keeping of district TESOL specialists. It will be essential to make contact with these district-level coordinators, to gain their perspectives and support, to get their recommendations of specific schools that may be receptive, and to get references from them to key personnel at the school level.

Next, it is crucial for freelance storytellers and folklorists to develop partnerships in the schools in which they would like to plan a residency. Specifically the partnership should include allies at the administrative level (a principal or assistant principal), at the departmental level (the TESOL coordinator or department head), and the classroom level (a teacher or group of teachers who are willing to host the project).

With some basic preparation—including judicious use of this book—teachers alone can create valuable and productive units on family and ethnic traditions. But TESOL folklore projects are particularly effective when designed as collaborations between classroom teachers and a folklore or storytelling specialist who can bring a wealth of experience and host of examples to spark students' imaginations. If you are a classroom teacher or administrator who would like to initiate such a collaboration, most state and local arts council have rosters and registries of experienced storytellers and folklorists who are available to work in schools. You may find several on these lists whose work would seem compatible with the goals of the intended project. Get in touch to sound them out.

Another useful resource is the National Task Force for Folk Arts in Education. It keeps a Web site called Cultural Arts Resources for Teachers and Students, or CARTS (http://www.carts.org). This site is full of references for folklorists and folk artists, articles and suggested books, and training opportunities all around the nation for teachers interested in bringing local cultures into the classroom.

If you are an independent professional storyteller or folklorist, you probably have some experience with the research involved in marketing to schools and other community organizations. For specific projects of this type it is advisable to go to a city or district office to seek out the district-level TESOL coordinator, and to gather as much demographic survey information as you can about the particular TESOL populations at each secondary school in the district. This will help you select the most promising sites to propose your residency, and it will help give you a common language to speak with administrators and with TESOL teachers and coordinators at the school level as you present your project to them.

TESOL folklore projects can be carried out on a volunteer basis, but more commonly a freelance artist or folklorist will need some kind of financial support. The manifest benefits of such a project make it a compelling candidate for grant support from a wide range of foundations, public agencies, and local school organizations. Because schools with large TESOL populations are often in low-income neighborhoods, these projects are likely recipients of Title One reading funds or grants specifically targeted to low-income populations. The Chicago Department of Cultural Affairs Neighborhood Arts Program, which supported most of my residencies in Chicago city schools, is one such program. City Lore in New York City is another organization that channels state and federal funding into traditional and ethnic arts programs in public schools. A little research will bring to light the relevant cultural agencies in your area. Local and regional arts councils, school boards and PTOs, community nonprofit foundations, and private businesses with school partnership programs are all potential sources of funding for a TESOL folklore project.

Folklore and story collecting projects can generally be carried out successfully with a wide range of age groups—potentially from fourth or fifth grade up. The students chosen to participate should be old enough to understand the distinctions between types of traditional stories—between fables and fairy tales, for example, or between ghost stories and trickster tales. They should also be able to understand the differences between personal experience stories (memoirs) and traditional fictions. Students younger than nine or ten are often unprepared to keep these distinctions in mind, at least not long enough to take them home and carry on successful interviews with their elders. Maintaining and communicating these distinctions in the interview process will be crucial to producing a coherent collection. There may be exceptional students who have the necessary maturity and motivation to do so at seven or eight, but developmental norms will usually inhibit large-scale projects like this until secondary school age.

On the other hand, elementary students make marvelous audiences for traditional folktales, and so should certainly be included as such in project applications where older student-collectors learn to retell their tales to the school community. They can also be carefully coached to conduct basic interviews with community elders, especially in classroom settings with a teacher, storytelling specialist, or folklorist present to help guide the interactions. Veteran teacher Paula Rogovin has made classroom interviewing a centerpiece of her multicultural education curriculum for her first-grade class, as described in her 1998 book, *Classroom Interviews: A World of Learning* (Chicago: Heinemann, 1998). With imagination and sensitivity, teachers can adapt the exercises in her book, and those in this one, to a variety of ages and curricular goals.

Projects like this are ideally conducted with third-year and fourth-year (transitional) TESOL students. At these levels, students will have had enough exposure to the mechanics of English speaking and writing to be capable of and comfortable with turning their attention to extended projects involving higher-level analytical and interactional skills. The folklore project in particular can be framed for students as a demonstration of linguistic and cultural mastery. When students can negotiate the demands of interviewing, documenting, and translating a range of speech genres from his or her first language community into an English-literate framework, it can function for them as a kind of TESOL honors thesis. It can help mark the transition from the second childhood of basic TESOL to the complex demands of the mainstream classroom.

Basic Competencies

Basic competencies that may be achieved by students through these activities will include (but are not limited to) the following:

1. Will experience the transmission of cultural values through community oral traditions.
2. Will appreciate the diversity of cultural traditions flourishing within students' own neighborhoods and school communities.
3. Will analyze the relationship between oral and literary traditions of various cultures through transcribing and editing oral interviews and crafting literary versions of oral tales.
4. Will develop skills in conducting interviews with community elders, using coherent qualitative fieldwork methods.
5. Will develop skills of cultural interpretation through recording tales and related cultural lore in their original languages and translating the lore into the cultural system of the English language.

How do TESOL teachers, folklorists, and storytellers make the case with beleaguered school administrators that this kind of project will help with and not detract from the pursuit of basic skills? Perhaps with the help of the following story, "Educated and Uneducated," which I received at Roosevelt High School from Nayan and Shailesh Patel, cousins from the Indian state of Gujarat. They learned it from their grandmother:

> In a village in India there were four Brahman families. The four sons of these families were very close friends. Then three of the sons went away to a distant country to get a better education. The fourth son stayed at home.
>
> The three sons who went abroad became very educated people. After several years they came home to their village, and there they met their old friend. He was overjoyed to see them again—but the three of them were very haughty and proud of their fine education.
>
> One day, for old time's sake, the four old friends took a walk in the jungle. As they walked they came to a pile of scattered bones. The first educated man said, "Let me see if I can make a complete skeleton out of this pile of bones." He went to work and soon he had a complete skeleton laid out before them. It was clearly the skeleton of a lion.
>
> The second educated man said, "Let me see if I can put muscles, blood, and flesh on those bones." He went to work with some mud and magic words, and soon he had surrounded those bones with muscles, blood, and flesh. The lion lay before them in all its magnificence—but dead.
>
> Not to be outdone, the third educated man said, "Let me see if I can put the breath of life into that body."
>
> Then the uneducated man spoke up. "Wait just a minute," he said. "I know that you are all very educated people and I am a simple country man. But don't you see that this here is the body of a lion? If you bring it to life he'll kill us."
>
> "This creature can't kill us," they explained. "We are protected by the power of our great education." Then the third educated man bent down and blew the breath of life into the lion's mouth.
>
> The uneducated man jumped into a tree and climbed straight to the top. From there he watched as the lion came to life and killed all three of his educated friends. More lions quickly gathered, and jackals, and vultures, and when they were all done feasting there was nothing left but a pile of scattered bones.
>
> Then the uneducated man climbed down from the tree. Gazing sadly at the pile of bones, he said, "If I only had their education, I'd know just what to do about this . . ."
>
> He sighed. "But I wouldn't be here to do it."

Traditional stories, proverbs, and other forms of cultural lore may seem simple and unrelated to the main educational enterprise of the public schools. But they are full of grounded common-sense values, character development, and rich themes for exercising critical thinking, pattern recognition, and empathy. In performing the work of collecting, transcribing, translating, and editing the products, students will in fact be developing and practicing their basic skills after all—only with the additional energy of personal and cultural involvement, investment, and revelation.

Priming the Pump

I always like to start a folklore project by telling stories. In part, that's just who I am as a performer and teacher. But there are sound pedagogical and practical reasons as well. Storytelling "primes the pump." It is entertaining *and* informative, and it models the kinds of cultural artifacts and activities that we are seeking without stress or strain on students' part. It may involve extra efforts on the teller or teachers' part, but the skill of the teller lies in concealing that effort!

So, in initial sessions of thirty minutes to an hour, tell (or have your participating storytelling specialist tell) a range of traditional story types:

- Short fables or teaching tales, like "You Can't Please Everybody" or "Educated and Uneducated."
- Legends of ghosts or the supernatural, like "La Llorona," "El Sombreron," or "The Ghost Pig."
- Fool tales, like "Juan Bobo's Pig" or "Nasruddin Prepares for Death."
- Trickster tales, like "The Dancing Tree" or "Anansi the Spider."
- Full-length wonder tales (also known as magic tales or fairy tales), like "The Youngest Son and the Queen of Beauty" or "The House Between Earth and Sky."

These or other related stories from your own or your participating storyteller's repertoire would be suitable to prime the pump and inspire students with the beauty, excitement, and enjoyment of what they are looking for in their own homes and neighborhoods. Be sure to prompt the students continually as you tell these introductory stories, with questions like, "Do you remember hearing stories like these as you were growing up? Can you think of anyone in your family or community who might know stories like these?"

Common Traditional Story Genres

Traditional stories are classified by folklorists into a number of *story genres*. Understanding these genres can give us a basic understanding of how these stories are shaped, and how they function in oral tradition. Bear in mind that these distinctions are fluid, not invariable. Oral traditional stories are constantly changing, and their generic markers can shift depending on context and on the skills, beliefs, and cultural needs of narrators and listeners. But folkloristic genres mark excellent starting places for analysis and discussion.

Fables are short, simply constructed fictional tales, often involving animal or other nonhuman characters, intended to drive home a point or lesson about how to live in the world.

Legends are stories of marvelous or frightening occurrences, believed to be true or possibly true, often spiced with localized references and verifying details (e.g., "Near the town where my mother grew up . . . " or "This happened to a friend of a friend . . ."). The telling of legends can be a way of declaring or exploring our beliefs about the world, or even a way of deciding what our beliefs really are.

Fool tales are humorous tales about a lovably simple-minded character whose laziness and misguided logic gets him (or her) into one jam after another.

Trickster tales are humorous tales about a character whose cleverness and agility of mind enable him (or her) to win out over stronger but less intelligent characters. Often, trickster tales, like the more simply constructed *fables,* feature animal characters with human traits (e.g., Rabbit, Fox, Spider, Raven, Monkey). *Fool tales* and *trickster tales* are closely related. Often the foolish hero wins out in the end because of his basic innocence, while the trickster hero loses out by being "too clever for his own good." Taken together, fool and trickster tales provide a spectrum of ethical images on themes of innocence and experience, incompetence and mastery.

Wonder tales (also known as *fairy tales*) are complex traditional stories centered around a young hero's journey in pursuit of fortune or a bride (or both), or a young heroine's journeys to deliver herself from evil or persecution. Wonder tales nearly always have as their hero or heroine a young man or woman, but within these tales, animals speak, horses fly, and semi-divine magical helpers grant special powers and gifts to help the hero or heroine on his or her way. Wonder tales take place in a landscape of supernatural figures and events, which are not told as literally true as in legends, but obey their own laws of formula and fantasy, from "Once upon a time . . . " to ". . . happily ever after."

Telling Tips

If you are new to storytelling, here are some things to remember.

- It is best not to try and memorize stories word for word, but to fix in your mind the sequences of action in the tales and to retell them in your own way, using as much animation, dialogue, and description as is natural to you. Let the students' attentiveness and their natural hunger for good stories draw the animation and energy out of you and into your performance.

- If oral performance of stories is truly not within the grasp of anyone connected with your project, the stories can be read aloud for demonstration purposes—again, with as much animation and naturalness as you can muster.

- Giving students stories to read on their own, whether from this book or from other folktale collections, is also appropriate, but only as additional examples, not as substitutes for actually hearing the tales. It is essential that students have the chance to practice listening to stories, both to improve their general listening skills and to be able to listen better to their elders tell their stories.

Each type of traditional story has its own natural form, its *story grammar,* that exists on a level of structure above the actual language in which it is told. Listening helps one grow accustomed to these formal story grammars and apply them across barriers of language and culture. It is this transcultural logic of traditional stories that has helped them to migrate from place to place, language to language, and to endure for hundreds, even thousands of years. And it is that same formal power that makes them such compelling material for students, allowing them to grow accustomed to thinking, feeling, and imagining in a new language system.

Storytelling and Folklore Resources

Art and Technique

Baker, Augusta, and Ellin Greene. *Storytelling: Art and Technique.* New York: Bowker, 1977.
Birch, Carol. *The Whole Story Handbook.* Little Rock, AK: August House, 2000.
Breneman, Lucille N., and Bren Breneman. *Once Upon a Time: A Storytelling Handbook.* Chicago: Nelson, 1983.
Collins, Rives, and Pamela Cooper. *The Power of Storytelling.* Scottsdale AZ: Gorsuch, 1992.
Davis, Donald. *Telling Your Own Stories.* Little Rock, AK: August House, 1992.
———. *Writing as a Second Language.* Little Rock, AK: August House, 2000.

Lipman, Doug. *Improving Your Storytelling*. Little Rock, AK: August House, 2000.
———. *The Storytelling Coach*. Little Rock, AK: August House, 1995.
Livo, Norma J., and Sandra A. Rietz. *Storytelling: Process and Practice*. Littleton, CO: Libraries Unlimited, 1986.
MacDonald, Margaret Read. *The Storyteller's Start-up Book*. Little Rock, AK: August House, 1993.
O'Callahan, Jay. *A Master Class in Storytelling*. West Tisbury, MA: Vineyard Video, 1983.
Pellowski, Anne. *The World of Storytelling*. New York: Bowker, 1977.
Ross, Ramon Royal. *Storyteller*, 4th ed. Little Rock, AK: August House, 1998.
Rubright, Lynn. *Beyond the Beanstalk: Interdisciplinary Learning through Storytelling*. Chicago: Heinemann, 1996.
Sawyer, Ruth. *The Way of the Storyteller*. New York: Viking, 1942.
Shedlock, Marie. *The Art of the Storyteller*. New York: Dover, 1951.
Yolen, Jane. *Touch Magic*. Little Rock, AK: August House, 2000.

Bibliographies and Storytelling Sourcebooks

Aarne, Antti. *The Types of the Folk-tale: A Classification and Bibliography,* trans. Stith Thompson. New York: Lenox, 1928.
Greene, Ellin, and George Shannon. *Storytelling: An Annotated Bibliography*. New York: Garland, 1986.
Iarusso, Marilyn. *Stories: A List of Stories to Tell and to Read Aloud,* 7th ed. New York: New York Public Library, 1977.
MacDonald, Margaret Read. *The Storyteller's Sourcebook: A Subject, Title and Motif Index to Folklore Collections for Children*. Detroit: Neal/Gale, 1982.
Norton, Donna E. *Through the Eyes of Many Children: Multicultural Children's Literature*. Saddle River, NJ: Prentice Hall, 2000.
Shannon, George W. B. *Folk Literature and Children: An Annotated Bibliography of Secondary Materials*. Westport, CT: Greenwood, 1981.

Folkore, History and Repertoire

Abrahams, Roger, ed. *African Folktales*. New York: Pantheon, 1983.
———. *Afro-American Folktales*. New York: Pantheon, 1985.
Afanasyev, Alexandr. *Russian Fairy Tales*. New York: Pantheon, 1976.
Aesop. *Aesop's Fables,* ed. D. L. Ashliman. New York: Barnes and Noble Classics, 2003.
Bierhorst, John, ed. *Latin American Folktales*. New York: Pantheon, 2003.
Bruchac, Joseph. *Tell Me a Tale*. New York: Harcourt Brace, 1997.
Bruchac, Joseph, and Michael Caduto. *Keepers of the Earth*. Golden, CO: Fulcrum, 1988.
Bushnaq, Inea, trans. and ed. *Arab Folktales*. New York: Pantheon, 1986.
Calvino, Italo, ed. *Italian Folktales*. New York: Harcourt, 1980.
Chase, Richard, ed. *American Folk Tales and Songs*. New York: New American Library, 1956.
———. *Grandfather Tales*. Boston: Houghton, Mifflin 1948.
———. *The Jack Tales*. Boston: Houghton, Mifflin 1943.
Cole, Joanna. *Best-Loved Folktales of the World*. Garden City, NY: Anchor, 1983.
Courlander, Harold. *Fire on the Mountain, and other Ethiopian Folktales*. Holt, Rinehart, 1950.
Curtin, Jeremiah. *Hero Tales of Ireland*. 1894; repr., New York: Blom, 1971.
———. *Myths and Folk Tales of Ireland*. 1890; repr., New York: Dover, 1975
Davis, Donald. *Southern Jack Tales*. Little Rock, AK: August House, 1992.
Dorson, Richard. *Buying the Wind*. Chicago: University of Chicago Press, 1964.
Erdoes, Richard, and Alphonso Ortiz, eds. *American Indian Myths and Legends*. New York: Pantheon, 1985.

Glassie, Henry, ed. *Irish Folktales*. New York: Pantheon, 1985.

Grimm, Jacob, and Wilhelm Grimm. *Complete Fairy Tales*. New York: Pantheon, 1944.

Hamilton, Martha, and Mitch Weiss. *How and Why Stories*. Little Rock, AK: August House, 1999.

Hassan, Mohammed. *The Wise Coward Man*. Stockholm: Peppercorn, 2002.

Holt, David, and Bill Mooney. *More Ready-to-Tell Tales*. Little Rock, AK: August House, 1999.

———. *Ready-to-Tell Tales*. Little Rock, AK: August House, 1994.

Hyde, Douglas. *Beside the Fire*. London: Nutt, 1890.

MacDonald, Margaret Read. *Peace Tales*. Little Rock, AK: August House, 1992.

McDermott, Gerald. *The Stonecutter*. London: Puffin, 1978.

National Storytelling Association. *Many Voices: Stories from America's Past*. NSA, Jonesborough, Tennessee, 1994. Book and teachers' guide.

National Storytelling Association. *Tales as Tools: The Power of Story in the Classroom*. NSA, Jonesborough, Tennessee, 1994.

National Storytelling Press. *Favorite Stories from the National Storytelling Festival*, 1991.

Opie, Iona, and Peter Opie. *The Classic Fairy Tales*. London and New York: Oxford University Press, 1974.

Oring, Elliott, ed. *Folk Groups and Folklore Genres: An Introduction*. Logan: Utah State University Press, 1986.

———. *Folk Groups and Folklore Genres: A Reader*. Logan: Utah State University Press, 1989.

Ramanujan, A. K. *Folktales from India*. New York: Pantheon, 1991.

Ryder, Arthur W. *Panchatantra*. Chicago: University of Chicago Press, 1964.

Schram, Peninnah. *Stories within Stories: From the Jewish Oral Tradition*. Northvale, NJ: Jason Aronson, 2000.

Schwartz, Howard. *Gabriel's Palace*. London: Oxford University Press, 1994.

Shah, Idries. *The Pleasantries of the Incredible Mullah Nasrudin*. New York: Dutton, 1971.

———. *Tales of the Dervishes*. New York: Dutton, 1970.

———. *World Tales*. New York: Harcourt Brace, 1979.

Smith, Jimmy Neil. *Homespun*. New York: Crown, 1988.

Somadeva, Bhatta. *The Ocean of Story,* trans. C. H. Tawney. Delhi: Motilal Banarsidass, 1968.

Thompson, Stith. *The Folktale*. New York: Dryden, 1946.

Toelken, Barre. *The Dynamics of Folklore*. Logan: Utah State University Press, 1996.

The Storytelling Revival

Birch, Carol, and Melissa Heckler. *Who Says? Essays on Pivotal Issues in Contemporary Storytelling*. Little Rock, AK: August House, 1996.

Sobol, Joseph D. *The Storytellers' Journey: An American Revival*. Urbana: University of Illinois Press, 1999.

2. WEEK TWO: PROVERBS AND BELIEFS

Bolje ista nego nista. (Better something than nothing)

—Bosnian proverb

The building that is Nicholas Senn High School is one of the architectural gems of the Chicago city system. The main wing, constructed in 1913, is an educational palazzo, with a white brick and terra cotta facade showing the whole range of neoclassical ornamentation—ceremonial steps, Corinthian columns, pediment and cornice—still magnificent, even if crumbling in places and bedecked with scaffolding. The builders were clearly thinking of Greece, Rome, London, Paris, of the capitals of all the great empires of the world. They were proud to provide for the students of this North Side Chicago neighborhood a building that claimed a place for them in that imperial tradition.

Now, at the end of the century, this building, this neighborhood, this city, and this country have a very different set of challenges flowing through them. The imperial aspirations that were still very much potential when the building was new are now long-established fact. The world may be fast becoming a village stamped with American trademarks, but this school, its neighborhood, and its city have at the same time become a global frontier.

There are students from as many as fifty-eight countries attending Senn in any given year. The halls are a forest ringing with African, Asian, Latin American, and urban American dialects. Wherever there is economic, political, or natural disaster or disorder in the world, from thence one can expect to find students arriving at Senn, often speaking little or no language but what their mothers taught them. During this year of 1998–1999, the school welcomed its first group of Kosovar Albanians. There will be more. And so it goes in the Senn TESOL and Multilingual Department.

Hot Pepper and Boiling Water

Students in places like Senn, just by virtue of their own life stories, are in training to be cultural interpreters. Whether they know it or like it or try their best to hide it, they will always be interpreting their ways to mainstream America and interpreting the ways of mainstream America to their families and to themselves.

Folklore and storytelling offer powerful tools to make this process work. The discipline of folklore says that there are patterns in the ways different peoples view the world and express their worldview. Reduced to basics, folklore offers the hope that if we show one another our cultural treasures, a measure of our common humanity may dawn. Similarly, a central article of faith in the contemporary revival of storytelling holds that many of the beautiful, mysterious, hilarious, frightening, and enlightening things about people and their cultures are open and accessible through sharing one another's stories. I would add that these are intentional processes, which when performed in good faith, bring desirable results for individuals, for groups, and for society. Even limited efforts, as at Senn, can reveal some remarkable treasures.

I began my residency at Senn at the end of the 1998–1999 school year, under the auspices of the Chicago Department of Cultural Affairs Neighborhood Arts Program, spending the last three weeks of the semester in the advanced ESL classrooms of Drue Hoffman and Theresa Pratt. The school was on academic probation because of low standardized test scores, and the entire place was on a kind of basic-skills lockdown lest unthinkable consequences fall from above. Thus, of the entire TESOL faculty at Senn, only these two teachers had the serene self-assurance to yield their classrooms and surrender precious instructional time to the project. It was a difficult period for the school, and for me. My mother lay dying in California. I flew out to say good-bye to her and returned from her bedside to complete the residency. In September and October of 1999, I went back to Senn for a few weeks to edit and arrange the material into a booklet for the school. I also reinterviewed students and collected a fair amount of additional material, which was still coming in when the deadline for the grant report came along and shut the lid.

I am certain that I managed to draw only a teacup out of an ocean of traditional tales and cultural wisdom that flows through Senn's halls. With just a week to go before the project had to be wrapped, a girl came into the computer lab where I was typing up stories. When I asked where her family was from, she said that they were from Brazil. When I asked if she had heard traditional stories growing up, her face lit up. Yes, she said, her grandmother had been from an Amazon Indian tribe and told her many beautiful stories from the sacred myths of that people. She promised to write some of them down for me. But there was not enough time left to receive and edit them for the book. She, like so many others at Senn and in the ethnic communities of Chicago and other cities, hold these folkloristic treasures inside, to be shared with the rest of us, or not—but just waiting for the right invitation to open the gates.

One day as I sat in the ESL lab between classes, two beautiful sisters, Olumayakun and Bosede Osinubi from Nigeria, came in and told me the story "Hot Pepper and Boiling Water." It was entrancing to hear and watch them sing and dance the Tortoise's refrain.

Hot Pepper and Boiling Water

Once upon a time there was a king who had a beautiful daughter. All the men in the kingdom wanted her for a wife. But the king put out word that only the one who could eat hot pepper and drink boiling water could marry his daughter.

Lion tried, but he burnt his mouth and ran away home. Leopard tried, but he couldn't stand it either. Hippopotomus tried, and he ate and drank every bit—then half an hour later he keeled over dead. All the animals tried and failed. Finally it was Tortoise's turn.

Tortoise put the hot pepper in his mouth. Then he raised the pitcher of boiling water to his lips and he began to dance!

"Hambo-amoday shuriale, su! (ssss-ssss) Su ya-ya!" which means, roughly, "Dance with me, children, all night long! Boogie, yeah, yeah, yeah!"

Every time he sang *"ssss-ssss!"* Tortoise sucked in cool air along with a sip of the water. And he kept on dancing so he wouldn't notice the pain from the hot peppers.

"Hambo-amoday shuriale, su (ssss-ssss)! Su ya-ya!"

And all the people there sang and danced with Tortoise, till he had drunk all the boiling water and eaten all the hot pepper. And that's how Tortoise married the king's daughter.

Making a go of life in a new society can be a bit like eating hot pepper and drinking boiling water—only those who can keep singing and dancing through the inevitable distress will get to marry the new king's daughter. I wish all these students the wit and wisdom of Tortoise.

Proverbs

Proverbs are the palm oil with which words are eaten.

—African proverb

After the introductory period of priming the pump with stories, songs, folk dances, or other traditional performances, I find it useful to initiate students into the practice of folklore collecting with proverbs. Proverbs are the shortest and most portable genre of verbal folk art. They are present in abundance in virtually every language. When students begin actively looking for proverbial expressions, it can be like looking for dandelions or lightning bugs—they suddenly start turning up everywhere.

Proverbs can be defined as traditional sayings that carry a lesson or generate meaning with maximum compression and maximum expression. They accomplish this by employing the devices of oral poetry:

- rhyme—repetition of vowel/consonant combinations, as in *Haste makes waste*.
- alliteration—repetition of initial consonant sounds, as in *Curiosity killed the cat*.
- assonance—repetition of interior vowel sounds, as in *The early bird gets the worm*.
- rhythm—patterns of accented and unaccented syllables, as *in The devil is in the details*.
- formal symmetry—a balanced two-part structure, as in *Better late than never*.
- metaphor—use of concrete images to evoke complex meanings, as in *You can lead a horse to water, but you can't make him drink*.

All of these techniques come packed into tight linguistic frames in order to concentrate mnemonic power. Proverbs are verbal formulas that are meant to be stored away for life, to spring to mind whenever they are needed.

It can be safely assumed that the more orally based the culture, the more plentiful proverbs will be. While there are many proverbs still current in English, there are likely to be more of them in wider use in Mexican Spanish, Bosnian Serbo-Croatian, Urdu, Akan, and Yoruba. One Indian student at Roosevelt High School, Saiyada Maria, turned in a collection of some 334 Urdu proverbs she put together with the help of her father. Many orally-based educational systems still make memorization of proverbs a basis of the curriculum. The Book of Proverbs in the Old Testament is precisely that: a written record of the accumulated oral wisdom of the tribe. In some African tribal cultures, the training of legal scholars in the resolution of disputes still relies upon proverbs—he who can best cite and interpret proverbs to illuminate the case at hand will be judged the victor. Such are the prestige and plentitude of these traditional formulas in traditional societies.

I find that when the rules and defining characteristics of proverbs are explained to students, they get very quickly excited, foraging through their linguistic memory banks to uncover examples of their own. It is as if they have been reminded of a treasure they had only dimly suspected lay hidden in their own minds. This is precisely the feeling that we want to engender in relation to other kinds of folklore (and in relation to the entire educational enterprise!), but it is kindled most immediately by the genre of proverbs.

Examples of Proverbs

The following proverbs were collected by students in the Chicago schools. They are accompanied by literal English translations.

Mexican

Ojos que no ven, corazon que no siente.
(Eyes that won't see, heart that won't feel.)

De tal palo tal astilla.
(From such a pole, such a splinter; or, Chip off the old block.)

Si el palo se le mete al ocho en el ocho se dura.
(The pole that gets stuck at eight stays at eight.)

Camoron que se duerme, se lo lleva la corriente.
(Sleeping shrimp drift with the tide.)

Agua que no has de beber, dejala correr.
(Water you don't drink, let it go.)

Arbol que nace chueco sirve para columpio.
(The twisted tree makes a good swing.)

Arbol q'nace torcido jamos endereza.
(The tree born crooked never grows straight.)

Al mejor casador se le va la leibre.
(To the best hunter goes the hare.)

Mas sabe el diablo por viejo que por diablo.
(The devil has learned more from being old than from being the devil.)

Cuando el gato sale los ratones hacen fiesta.
(When the cat's away, the mice have a fiesta.)

En casa de jabonero el que no cae resbala.
(In the soapmaker's house, even those who don't fall stumble.)

En casa de herrero puerta de palo.
(In the blacksmith's house, doors of wood.)

Donde hubo fuego, cenizas quedan.
(Where there was fire, ashes remain.)

Hierba mala nunca muere.
(Crabgrass never dies.)

De tragones y glotones estan llenas los panteones.
(The graveyards are full of gourmands.)

Mas rapido cae un hablador que un cajo.
(A talker falls faster than a cripple.)

La mona auque se vista de seda, mona se queda.
(A monkey in silk is a monkey all the same.)

Limosnero con garrote.
(A beggar with a billyclub.)

De la mano a la boca se puerde la sopa.
(Between the hand and the mouth the soup is spilled.)

Quien canta sus males espanta.
(He who sings scares off sorrow.)

El que no corre vuela.
(If you can't run, fly.)

El que anda con lobos a aullar se ensena.
(He who runs with the wolves learns to howl.)

Los ninos y los borrachos siempre dicen la verdad.
(Children and drunks always tell the truth.)

Hablando del Rey de Roma, por la puerta se asoma.
(Speak of the King of Rome, he'll show up at your home.)

Bosnian

Bolje ista nego nista.
(Better something than nothing.)

Vrana vrani oci nevadi.
(Crows don't peck another crow's eye.)

Na muci se posnaju junaci.
(The worst of times brings out the greatest of heroes.)

Ko rano rani, dvije srece grabi.
(The early riser grabs two fortunes.)

Ko drugom jamu kopa, sam u nju pada.
(He who digs a hole for another falls in himself.)

Pametnij popusta.
(The wise one surrenders.)

Tko nema u glavi, ima u nogama.
(What he lacks in the head, he makes up in the legs.)

Bolje Sprijeciti nego lijeciti.
(Better prevention than cure.)

Covjek se uci dok je ziv.
(Learn as long as you live.)

Nekom lose zelio, lose ti se vratilo.
(Ill wishes return to their sender.)

Arabic

الجنون يكي دالعائلي يـَمَـغ

Al-majnoon yahkee, wal-aqel yasmaa.
(The fool talks, the wise one listens.)

ن حفر بئرا لأخيه, وقع فيه

Men hafara bearan lakhee-hee waqaa fee-hee
(Who digs a hole for his brother falls in himself.)

الديك الفصيح من البيضة يصيح

Al-deek al faseeh min al-baidha yaseeh.
(The wise turkey screams from the egg.)

Albanian

Fjalet jane argjend, heshtja eshte flori.
(Words are silver, silence is gold.)

Somalian

Af dawoolan wa dahab.
(A quiet mouth is golden.)

Vietnamese

Con cóc là câu ông trời, ai dánh cóc thì trời dánh cho.
(Hit a frog, God hits you back.)

Cambodian

ចេះមកពីរៀន បានមកពីរក

Knowing comes from learning, and having comes from finding.

Gujarati

જીવન ટૂંકુ છે કામ ઘણા છે

Javan tuku she, kama gana she.
(Life is short, art is long.)

સત્ય નો માર્ગ કઠણ છે

Satya no marg kathan che.
(The road of truth is rough.)

Urdu

اچھا کرے خدا، ناآ ڈ اکٹر کا

Acha karay khuda naam doctor ka.

God cures, the doctor takes the credit.

اپنا پوت پریا ڈھینگر

Apna poot puriya dhengur.

Each man thinks his own geese are swans.

انت ،بھلے کا بھلا

Unt bhalay ka bhala.
The end crowns all.

Folklore Project Assignment 1

Teachers should give out this assignment toward the end of Week 1, giving students the weekend to collect the lore and hand it in on Monday.

Interview Question: What proverbs, or short, memorable phrases can you remember people saying as you were growing up to express a commonplace truth or wisdom about living? Give your interview subject some examples from the list of proverbs to help him or her understand what you are looking for.

Thought Exercises

1. Some of the translations of the international proverbs also have proverb status in English. For others, the equivalent English proverbs are different—sometimes subtly, sometimes more distinctly. See if you can find the English proverbial equivalent for these. For example, the proverbial English equivalent for the Spanish proverb *Hablando del Rey de Roma, por la puerta se asoma* would be . . . ?

2. Study the devices of oral poetry (rhyme, alliteration, assonance, rhythm, formal symmetry, and metaphor). Then pick a selection of proverbs in English and in your own first language. See how many of these techniques you can identify in each.

3. What are some key differences between proverbs and other compact speech genres such as idioms, popular catchphrases, and tongue twisters?

4. Oftentimes proverbs are used as the conclusion or moral of a story or fable. Can you think of any stories from your own culture in which this is the case? (Examples from Aesop's fables)

5. Pick a proverb that you remember from your own first language and describe the context in which it might be used. What kinds of situations might call this proverb to mind?

Beliefs and Customs

Beliefs are mental facts, culturally determined ways of viewing and interpreting the world. Beliefs permeate every cultural environment, and they give that environment much of its structure, texture, and flavor. Customs are refinements of beliefs into practices freighted with cultural obligation. When there is a sense that a cultural practice must be performed in the prescribed manner or else a variety of negative consequences may ensue, it can be assumed that we are moving into the realm of belief. Beyond those obligatory practices, there are also speculative beliefs and customs that seek to define the borders of the known world—those shadow zones where magic, imagination, and the unknown future come fleetingly into focus.

Beliefs can be so much a part of our inner landscape that they become invisible to us, though they are visible to anyone who looks at us from a different point of view. We tend to think of beliefs we have grown up with as normal and natural, while beliefs that people of other backgrounds grow up with may strike us as bizarre or, literally, outlandish. We may instinctively refer to other people's (or our own grandparents') beliefs as superstitions, while taking our own beliefs and assumptions for granted.

Although the word "superstition" often comes up in discussion, folklorists usually discourage its use. We lean toward the words "belief" and "custom" as more neutral, less pejorative. The purpose of this next assignment is not to evaluate or judge, but simply to collect and observe beliefs that come from a variety of cultural backgrounds, and to analyze how these beliefs become the basis of stories and customs. Because while traditional stories often end in proverbs, they are likely to begin with beliefs.

Beliefs usually cluster around matters of greatest concern to individuals or their family. Hence the great number of cultural beliefs related to bringing good fortune to oneself or bad fortune to one's enemies, and the prevalence of charms or formulas to bring about love or to guard against the evil eye. Beliefs about the supernatural, or, more accurately perhaps, about the margins between the seen and unseen worlds, are also nearly universal in oral traditions and are a failsafe way of getting the conversation on cultural beliefs started.

For example, the figure of La Llorona, the Wailing Woman, is not simply a colorful story to Latin American (particularly Mexican and Mexican-American) children; it is a belief, a part of the emotionally binding landscape of night. She is not alone there, however—she dwells alongside the Ciguanaba, a beautiful woman with one horse foot and one rooster foot who waits along the roads for drunken men, or El Sombreron, the Devil himself in a wide-brimmed hat. Black cats may have lost some of their power to chill, but in Vietnam the voice of an owl nearby may still signal impending death, and after death, a knife or a piece of steel may still be placed upon the corpse's chest to keep it from growing restless. In the Middle East, an amulet in the form of a stylized hand is worn to guard against the evil eye, and in many areas of the world coffee grounds at the bottom of a cup, in the hands of a skillful reader, can foretell your future.

Many students will reply to the probes below with orthodox ideas, whether Christian, Muslim, Jewish, Buddhist, Hindu, or Sikh. Others will struggle to find words for images and practices that are difficult to convey in any language, let alone an unfamiliar one. It is important to let students know, and to the best of your ability to make it real, that there will be no scale of better or worse, true or false in this assignment, as long as it is attempted in good faith.

Of course we can never reach a perfection of objectivity—if that is even a desired ideal—but we need to be able to grant at least a theoretical validity to every cultural idea beneath the sun if we are to allow our immigrant students' rich storehouses of heritage a place in the folklore classroom. In the end, our own points of view, like those of our students, are works in progress, subject to revision and exposed to fierce forces of assimilation and change. This way of articulating the process gives students space to perform some of their revisions publicly, with a structure that fosters appreciation and openness as well as critical and comparative thinking.

The tasks for students in Folklore Project Assignment 2 should be given to them to bring home and ask their elders—one, two, or as many generations back as they can reach. Gently encourage but do not force your students to dwell on customs and beliefs that are distinctive from mainstream American practice. If their need is to focus on similarities with their new neighbors rather than differences, that should be their right. We try to catch them at this particular point in their journeys so that looking back at older worlds will be as natural and necessary as looking forward.

Folklore Project Assignment 2

1. Report on a belief or custom from your family, community, or country of origin concerning something a person can do, say, make, wear, carry, and so forth that can produce one or more of the following effects:

   Bring good luck

   Bring bad luck

   Bring love or romance

   Cause harm to an enemy (by non-physical means)

   Protect oneself or one's family from harm (by non-physical means)

   Foretell the future

2. Report on a belief or custom from your family, community, or country of origin concerning a supernatural creature, such as a ghost, goblin, *duende* (Latin American elves or "little people"), *ciguanaba* (see p. 22), La Llorona (see p. 22), *wahash* (see p. 84), *djinn* (see p. 90), or *abwateia* (see p. 106).

3. Report on a custom or practice in your family, community, or country of origin that takes place around a holiday or special annual festival or event, for example, gift-giving, feast or fast, interior or exterior decoration, costuming, ritual, or celebration. Can you explore and explain the beliefs on which this practice is based?

3. WEEKS THREE AND FOUR: REMEDIES, RECIPES, CRAFTS, AND STORIES

The bell here at Mather High School is really not a bell, but a long, loud, electronic hoot. Before it finishes, all doors are flung open and the narrow halls fill with students and teachers—everyone streaming from room to room through the pressurized gap of a four-minute timeslot. The colors of this people-flood are wondrous. Just about every shade that God made and His children have bred or woven to cover their nakedness flashes by in the tumult, along with fanfares from a multitude of tongues.

The languages spoken in the halls of Mather are like a trip on a microcosmic Orient Express. Bursts of Russian, Ukrainian, Romanian, Bulgarian, Serbo-Croatian, Albanian, Turkish, Assyrian, Arabic, Urdu, Punjabi, Gujarati, Hindi, and Malayalam, with quick dips down into North and East Africa, onward to Vietnam, China, Korea, the Philippines, and back around through the New World colonies of Spain to this capitol of a global diaspora, the city of Chicago. To the ordinary identity crises of high school life, try adding these: Most students here are between languages, between cultures, between nationalities. Bosnian Serb, Croat, and Muslim, Kosovar Albanian, Romany, and Serb, Indian Hindu, Muslim, and Sikh may sit side by side in ESL classes, studying to be first-generation Americans. They are cultural pioneers, some by choice but most by accidents of fortune, or in the wake of far-distant catastrophes.

On the night of Ethnic Fest at Mather, spectators fill the bleachers on one side of the gym while rows of empty chairs line the other three sides. Then, at a signal, the parade begins. Each

of the ethnic clubs files in, decked in costumes from across the planet. They pass the bleachers and make the entire circuit of the gym before settling in their sections and waiting their turn to do a dance representing a people. Yet, look closely and you will see that the ethnic presentations are not uniform or simple—there are Philippinos in the French club, Koreans in the Japanese and Chinese clubs, Punjabi Sikhs in the Pakistani club. A Cuban boy dances the cross-armed Cossack squat-kicks of the Ukrainian club. High up along the walls hang not the retired jerseys of basketball stars, but eighty national flags on permanent exhibition. And when the performances are done, the clubs parade out again to the strains of Ray Charles singing "America."

I'm left thinking, this is really it—the America that politicians boast about (or rail against), preachers preach about, teachers teach about, editors editorialize and poets perorate about, and statues of liberty light their lamps to illumine. But this is none of that high-toned, grown-up fussing—this is it, the thing itself, in all its spectacle of adolescent becoming. Anyone who fails to be moved by this, as the saying goes, is in need of CPR.

The House Between Earth and Sky

I was at Mather High School on a visitor's pass, a grant from the Chicago Department of Cultural Affairs, for the fourth in a series of folklore workshops in the Chicago public schools. In April and May, 2000, I worked as a visiting artist with a number of ESL classes, teaching units on cultural traditions, beliefs, and proverbs, and especially on traditional folktales. I started the residency, as always, by meeting with teachers to determine a schedule and a program according to the available time and resources of the school. In the classroom, I began by telling a variety of stories in English from North American and international oral traditions to get students accustomed to the style and content of oral tales. Then I gave out collecting assignments along with guidelines for conducting folklore and oral history interviews.

The students collected stories, proverbs, beliefs, and other forms of traditional lore from family, friends, and neighbors in their ethnic communities. In the third week, the collection of stories began to come together. The students worked with me in the computer lab to put their collections down on disk, making it much easier to edit into a final product. In the fourth week, the week of Ethnic Fest, I did coaching work with some of the classes on performing their stories, in English as well as in their original languages. Whoever had the desire and the nerve had the chance to participate in the Ethnic Storytelling Center that became part of the official daylong Ethnic Fest celebration.

After that, I settled down in the computer lab to finish selecting, editing, and arranging the stories. There were many marvelous folktales collected by students in the Mather ESL Project, but one in particular, "The House Between Earth and Sky," stands out for me. It was turned in by Andrea Abidinovic, a sophomore, whose family had come from Bosnia. "This is an old story," she wrote, "told to me by an old lady that lives near my house. When this elderly lady was around eight years old she had a neighbor, an old lady that used to take care of a lot of neighborhood kids, and she used to tell them all these stories."

I recognized the story as an unusually full and colorful version of a classic European wonder tale. I had heard parallel versions told by my friends and storytelling mentors from the mountains of North Carolina, whose ancestors had left England, Scotland, and Germany centuries ago. Now I was reading an equally fine version, recorded by a fifteen-year-old girl whose parents and neighbors had only left Bosnia in the past decade, narrowly escaping a catastrophe of intolerance that had consumed their society. She had heard it from an old Bosnian woman in her North Side neighborhood, who had heard it in her youth from another old woman in Srebrenica or Sarajevo, in an ancient neighborhood that was now in ruins. And here it was, sprouting for me like a rare wildflower from a crack in a Chicago sidewalk.

Once upon a time there were six children, three boys and three girls, who lived alone with their mother. Everything was fine for them, but then she died. And when she died, the kids had to be responsible for their own lives. The girls started to grow up and to think about marriage, even though their older brothers were against it. The youngest brother, whom everyone thought of as a little bit slow, didn't mind if his sisters wanted to get married or not, because he just wanted them to be happy.

One day a young man came down the road and he asked for the hand of the oldest sister. She asked her brothers, "Who will give me away, since our parents are dead?" The two older brothers wouldn't give her away, because they wanted to have all their sisters around the house to do the chores and cook their dinners. But the youngest, the one who everyone thought was slow, said, "Sure, I'll give you away, 'cause I just want you to be happy." So the oldest girl got married and moved away.

A few months later, another young man came down the road and asked for the hand of the second sister. She turned to her brothers and asked, "Who will give me away, since our parents are both dead?" And again the two brothers wouldn't do it. But again the youngest brother agreed to give her away, because he just wanted her to be happy. And so she got married and moved away.

Then a few months later, another young man came down the road and asked for the hand of the youngest sister. Again the two brothers refused to give her away, but the youngest brother did, and she was married and moved away.

Now the two older boys were very angry with their brother. "Who will do the chores and cook and clean and make our lives easy?" they asked. "Not you, that's for sure. So you can go, too." And they threw their slow-witted brother out of the house.

He wandered down the road without any destination in mind till he came to a house that was not on the ground, and not in the sky, but in between. There was a man inside the house that called him. He walked up to the house without hesitation, because he had a simple heart. He entered and there he saw the oldest sister with her husband. They welcomed him and told him he could stay as long as he wanted.

He stayed there for one week, but then he said, "I don't want to wear out my welcome here. I should go home to my brothers—maybe they'll have forgiven me."

His sister said, "Don't forget to say goodbye to my husband. He will offer you whatever you want for a parting gift. Be sure to ask for the big iron pot on the topmost shelf. He'll tell you how to use it."

Sure enough, when he said goodbye to his brother-in-law, he was offered a parting gift, anything he could see. He asked for the big iron pot on the topmost shelf.

"Good choice," said the husband, "But if you take that pot you have to also take this strap. And every time you want something to eat, no matter what, just slap the strap against the pot, think about what you want, and you will get it."

"That's almost as good as a sister," he said, and he set out for his brothers' house to share his gift with them. At first they didn't want to let him in, but he pulled out the pot, slapped it with the strap, and made a beautiful feast for them.

They ate till they were stuffed, and once they were done, they all decided to visit the tavern. They were bragging about their magic pot, and the tavern keeper overheard their tale. So he kept on giving them free drinks till they agreed to bring the pot and show him how it worked.

The tavern keeper gave them a few more free drinks, till they all laid their heads on the table and fell asleep. Then the tavern keeper went in the back and switched the magic pot and strap for a set that had no magic in it. When the three boys got home they tried the magic pot to get some breakfast. When the older brothers saw that the pot wasn't working, they threw their youngest brother out again.

He walked and walked till he came to another house that was not on the ground and not in the sky, but in between. It was where his second sister lived with her husband. They invited him in and he was glad. He stayed with them for two weeks, and then he said, "I don't want to wear out my welcome here. I should go home to my brothers—maybe they'll have forgiven me."

His sister told him not to forget to say goodbye to her husband. And when he did, her husband would offer him a parting gift. "Remember to ask for the mule in the garden. He'll tell you what to do with it."

So that's what he did. "Good choice," said the husband. "And along with that mule you should take this bottle stopper. Whenever you're short of money, just put the bottle stopper in the mule's mouth, and out the other end will drop gold coins."

"That's almost as good as two sisters," he said, and he went straight home to show it to his brothers. They didn't want to let him in, but when he put the bottle stopper in the mule's mouth and it began dropping gold coins from its rear end, they changed their attitude. When the mule had made them a pretty good pile of money, they decided to go to the tavern again and celebrate. But the tavern keeper kept giving them free drinks till they'd given up the secret. Then after they had all passed out, the tavern keeper switched the magic mule and bottle stopper for an ordinary set. The next morning when the brothers tried to get some more money out of the mule, all he dropped was garden fertilizer.

"You won't fool us again," the older brothers said, and again they threw their youngest brother out of the house.

He walked and walked and walked till he came to yet another house that was not on the earth and not in the sky, but in between. It was the house of his youngest sister and her husband. He was so happy when they invited him to stay. But after he'd been there three weeks, he said, "I don't want to wear out my welcome here. I should go home to my brothers—maybe they'll have forgiven me."

His sister told him the same thing that he had heard from the other two. "When my husband asks what you want for a parting gift," she said, "don't forget to ask for that old leather purse hanging on the wall. He'll tell you how to use it."

The day he was leaving they made him a great feast, and the husband asked what the young man wanted for a gift. He said the old purse on the wall.

"Good choice," said the husband. "In that purse is a little purple genie who can do anything you want him to do. His name is Terbagider. Just call out his name—Terbagider—and whatever you ask of him he'll do. But when you've got what you asked for, you have to say, "Magider," which will make him go back in the purse. If you don't get him back in the purse, he'll turn on you, and then—watch out!"

"That's almost as good as three sisters," he said, and he went straight home to his brothers' house. "Look what I've got for us now!" he told them. "Terbagider!"

Out jumped the genie, and in a flash he built them a brand-new three-story house with a porch and all kinds of fancy work inside and out. "Let's celebrate!" the brothers cried, and again they went to the tavern and started getting drunk. But the tavern keeper was a little too greedy this time, and he exchanged purses before the younger brother had told the secret of how to get the genie back in the purse.

Once the tavern keeper had his hands on the magic purse he called out "Terbagider!" Out popped the genie and he completely remodeled the tavern. But when the genie was done he turned on the tavern keeper, jumped on his shoulders, and started beating him on the head with his little purple fists. "Help, help," the tavern keeper cried. "Get this devil off of me!"

The youngest brother opened one eye and mumbled, "First give us back our magic pot and strap, and our magic mule and bottle stopper."

"Anything you want," the tavern keeper cried. "Just stop this thing!"

He threw the youngest brother the magic purse. The youngest brother rose up on one elbow and shouted, "Magider!" In a flash the genie was back in the purse.

The brothers went home with all their magical gifts. All three brothers made excellent marriages, had many children, built many houses, and lived happily ever after.

—Bosnia (Mother)

High schools can be harsh, even dangerous terrain for students who are unprepared and culturally adrift. But at their best they can be something like a house between earth and sky. They can be places where young men and women, on the verge of being turned out of their childhood havens (or just emerging from its terrors), can find some temporary sanctuary and perhaps a few magical gifts—gifts of knowledge, skill, understanding, and self-assurance—that will help them feed themselves, earn a living, and build houses to hold their dreams.

Recipes

When new immigrants come to the United States, they often shed their language and other distinctive cultural markers even in the second generation. But traditional ethnic foodways can be much more persistent. Habits of the taste buds seem to stubbornly resist assimilation and to sustain pride of origins in ways language cannot. It may not be quite a universal language, but like music, food is easier to share with members of the surrounding culture than the immensely intricate frameworks embodied in words. So language is often sacrificed and traditional foods retained as a kind of negotiated cultural bargain with the new world. Ethnic restaurants in a city like Chicago are outposts of distant homelands. They are economic gateways into American society. And they are virtual conference centers where treaties are made between memories, ambitions, and appetites.

ESL students are usually excited to share the contents of their home kitchens with the school community. If the way to a man's heart is through his stomach, an easy shortcut to an ethnic culture is through its food. An activity involving food makes a fine centerpiece for a school-wide festival or international day. Make sure when bringing food into classrooms to check local regulations about food preparation, service, and storage.

Remedies

In areas of the world where medical supplies and personnel are scarce, a variety of traditional remedies develop over the generations to deal with common and uncommon ailments. These range from herbal treatments, such as teas and poultices, to cures that partake of the realms of faith and belief, such as prayer, amulets, and laying on of hands. There are people singled out by training and inclination to prescribe and provide these traditional remedies, and they sometimes carry a status within their communities akin to that of a mainstream medical doctor. There are also remedies and rituals that are more or less public domain, to which nearly everyone in a culture has access.

In areas like Chicago where traditional communities coexist with modern postindustrial society, people often hedge their bets, visiting medical clinics and hospitals when emergencies dictate and finances allow, but also persisting with certain traditional remedies and healing rituals when they are convenient and available. It is fascinating to inventory these customs in classes where students are gathered from around the world, to learn which ones endure in memory and which endure in practice.

Crafts

In modern society crafts are quaint refuges, recreations, and luxuries. Traditional crafts can be recreational as well and sources of beauty and serenity in austere circumstances. But they can also be essential parts of the fabric of traditional economic and social existence. That can be the case, literally, when we are talking about the weaving and sewing of cotton, linen, and wool for the making of clothing, bedding, and floor coverings, or figuratively, when we look at toolmaking and usage for farming, fishing, hunting, gathering, logging, woodworking, animal wrangling and riding, or other traditional occupations. Crafts can certainly incorporate aesthetic elements, such as in embroidery, quilting, rug making, or the making of musical instruments. Usually traditional crafts are characterized by a balance of aesthetic and functional considerations, as in furniture or pottery, the building of barns, or handmade fishing poles and lures. Crafts are often strongly gendered, divided into masculine and feminine domains. They are often attached to ritual and social occasions, such as the elaborate hand painted decoration of Easter eggs in Ukrainian culture, or the wedding calligraphies of Orthodox Jews or Pennsylvania Dutch. Contemporary folklorists often classify crafts under the larger heading of "material culture" and group them together with foodways and those aspects of folk medicine that draw on intimate knowledge and manipulation of the physical world.

Folklore Project Assignments 3–5 give students opportunities to explore the material folkways of their families and communities and to share them with their schoolmates in forms that can be smelled, tasted, and touched.

Folklore Project Assignments 3–5

3. Recipes

1. Can you share one or more of your favorite recipes for a traditional dish?

2. Are there particular special occasions when this dish (or dishes) is customarily served?

3. Is the dish still prepared the same way now as it was in your old home country? Are all of the traditional ingredients still available?

4. Are you or a family member able to prepare one of these dishes or a selection of them, and can you bring them in for us to try?

4. Remedies

1. What traditional cures or home remedies were used to help people when no medical doctor was available?

2. What conditions or ailments were they intended to treat?

3. How well did they work?

4. How were the remedies gathered, prepared, and administered?

5. Are some of those remedies still used today?

6. Were there traditional nonmedically trained doctors, *curanderos,* shamans, root workers, wise men or women, and so forth who especially knew these remedies? Are there still some active in this community?

5. Crafts

1. What traditional crafts (if any) were practiced in your family or community while you were growing up? Examples might include weaving, quilting, pottery, wood-carving, toy making, blacksmithing, memorial making, Easter egg painting, lace making, rug making, boat making, quilting or coverlet making, needlepoint, furniture making, and musical instrument making.

2. Are any of these crafts still practiced today?

3. Can you or anyone in your community be encouraged to come in and demonstrate it for our classes?

Story Collecting—A Step-by-Step Guide

Now we have reached the point in our folklore residency at which we are ready to assign the collecting of folktales (See Folklore Assignment 6). This is the culmination of the collecting phase of the project. Stories are the most extended form of folklore that we will deal with. There is great range and variability between folktale genres, from the brevity of fables to the episodic sweep of wonder tales, but because these latter can run to many pages of transcript, the students should be prepared to listen and to work more intensively with this assignment. Students may benefit from having an extra week or two (or even three) to complete the story interview and transcription.

The story interview should probably be conducted in the elder's first language. Unless the elder is fluent and comfortable in English, the native language will be the one in which the stories are most alive. Remind the students that the interviews should be conducted with a certain formality. Make an appointment with the elder. Make sure that there is enough time to talk without interruption or distraction. An hour is a good round figure. It may go longer (or shorter), but having sufficient time is a gift for both generations. Because of the additional scope of this assignment, at least a full extra week should be allowed for the students to complete it. It can even be useful to schedule the folklore unit to straddle a break such as Thanksgiving, Christmas, or Easter, to give students the chance to interact with family and neighbors during those very times when families naturally gather to rehearse their customs and traditions.

While students can usually collect the answers to the previous assignments fairly reliably on paper alone, it will be a great help—as several generations of folklorists have found—if they can be outfitted for story collecting with a portable cassette or mini-disk recorder. As it has for folklorists of every age and experience level, recording technology has made it possible for students to capture the exact language of their informants' tellings. When transcriptions from portable recording devices became the norm in folklore collecting, the entire field of storytelling study was transformed. Collections became more focused on the texture and artistry of traditional stories and of their performers, because the technology allowed us to listen back again and again and so to capture these nuances and details.

Be that as it may, it simply might not be possible to outfit all of your students with this kind of equipment—particularly in the inner city neighborhood schools where these residencies are most vitally needed. Because students in these neighborhoods are generally lower income, portable recording machines are not high on their families' lists of priorities, and the schools themselves will not have the items in bulk. Though grant proposals could conceivably be written specifically to address this lack, none of my Chicago residencies were graced with general availability of this most basic requirement of contemporary folkloristics. The result will most likely be that you will need to instruct your students in two media: the mechanics of the tape recorded interview and transcription process, and interviews using the quaint old-fashioned technology of written note taking.

For those students with access to recorders, you should take class time to do a demonstration. This can be done with great care and a certain tongue-in-cheek solemnity over the steps and the stature of the sacred technology. Nothing should be taken for granted, for each step in the technological process can be an occasion for a breakdown and the ruin of a perfectly auspicious interview. These steps include:

Preparing the machine. Remind the students that the recorder is their silent partner in the interview process, and that they will need to keep an eye on it to make sure it is doing its work.

Checking the power cord or the batteries. A cord and adaptor is preferable, but if batteries must be used, make sure to have spares on hand. Many an interview has been killed by a single set of dying batteries.

Demonstrating the basics of the control panel. Solemnly move through the stations of record, play, stop, fast forward, and rewind. Most students will be familiar with these things, but again, take nothing for granted.

Placing the microphone. This can be a sensitive matter. Most people with folk knowledge are not experienced media performers. Their comfort is crucial to the success of the interview. While it might be better for the sake of sound quality to have the microphone placed as close to the speaker as possible, or pinned to his or her lapel in the case of a lavolier mic, there can be an advantage to leaving the mic unobtrusively on the table between the interviewer and the speaker, where the nervous subject can temporarily forget its presence. If the mic is built into the recorder, as is often the case with inexpensive units, then this will be a moot point. But students should be reminded to keep the machine and the microphone close enough to both speaker and questioner throughout the interview so that all the words will be clear, and so that they can keep an eye on it to make sure that the wheels are still turning. Remind them that if they try to do an interview while chasing the subject around the kitchen, with the recorder sitting across the room, the sound quality will be all over the place as well, and transcribing will be a nightmare.

Taking care of the tape. Demonstrate the proper installation, use, and storage of the cassette or mini-disk. This means inserting it properly in the machine, checking to make sure it has not clicked off or filled up, replacing it when it is full (not turning the same cassette several times so that earlier material gets erased!), and labeling it thoroughly with names, dates, and identifying information so that the contents are not lost or recorded over. Demonstrate the record-protect or write-protect features on cassettes or mini-disks. Remind students of the gift that this interview material can provide for themselves and their families, now and in times to come. It is a way of preserving life, fragile and contingent as it may be. After their elders are gone, their words, their voices, their stories can remain.

When the interview is done and the tape or mini-disk is carefully labeled and stored, the next step will be the transcription. Transcribing is a painstaking and rather tedious process. It involves setting yourself up with the recorder and the word processor or notebook before you and moving back and forth between the play, stop, rewind, and fast forward buttons and the tools of writing, capturing one phrase or sentence at a time, checking back to see if you have written it down correctly, and going on to the next phrase. You can reasonably expect to spend an hour or so per page of text to get it completely right. The reward for this painstaking labor will be a written document that carries the flavor of the speaker's own language. The extra time invested in this stage of the process can save time later on, and it can also result in a richer, more characteristic end product.

The transcript in the original language will then be translated by the student into English. The handwritten or printed versions of stories in both the original language and the English translations should be handed in together to complete the assignment. Even if only the English versions are used in any eventual school publication, the precedence and dignity of the original language version should be maintained.

As I have already suggested, this sequence in its entirety is only a hopeful ideal. What is more likely—what was generally the case in my own Chicago residencies—is that most students will conduct their interviews with the age-old tools of pen and paper.

Tape recorders can do all the work of capturing the speakers' voices. They leave the interviewer's hands and eyes mostly free (except for the modest attention needed to keep the machine going), and they leave the grind work of transcribing for afterwards. But writing requires much more immediate labor from the interviewer. Because of this, students doing written interviews should be asked to coach their subjects to tell their favorite stories at least twice. For the first time, they should let the storyteller run uninterrupted, only taking notes on general story topics. When that interview is done, students should have a sense of which stories they want to hear again. They should be guided by their sense of folktale types and genres instilled from the start of the residency unit. During repeat performances, interviewers should take down the story in as much detail as they can, staying close to the storyteller's actual words. They should warn the teller that he or she may be asked to slow down, stop, or repeat something—knowing that the purpose is to produce a written version with as much detail as possible.

For all that, what is most likely to be turned in as the product of a pen-and-paper interview is a summary of a story rather than a complete performance transcript. My own experience is that there will be gaps in the stories that will need to be filled in to make them coherent. There will be abundant inconsistencies and errors of English grammar and usage that have little to do with the charms of oral traditional style. In the age of portable recording, it has become folkloristic orthodoxy to reproduce storytellers' words as precisely as technically possible. But in the actual conditions of these secondary TESOL residencies, in particular those that went into the making of this book, such documents as would compel that kind of fidelity largely do not exist. We are left with a range of complete and fragmentary text versions, and so the task of cobbling together consistent literary products becomes a collaboration between students and conscientious editors. While a few of the stories in Part 2 of this book are reproduced substantially as written down by the students, the bulk of the language in most of the stories is my own. Names of the student contributors can be found in Notes on the Stories at the back of the book.

Folklore Project Assignment 6

1. What stories do you remember hearing when you were growing up in your home community?

2. Who told the stories best? When—under what circumstances, places, times of day— would the stories be told?

3. Some types of stories to ask your elders about include:

   • Ghost stories or stories of encounters with supernatural creatures, fairies, omens, tokens of death, unusual sights or sounds, La Llorona, and so forth. These are legends—stories told as if they were true.

   • Stories of clever or foolish characters, like Jack, Juan Bobo, the Youngest Son, Nasruddin, Gioha or Hodja, Gopal, Birbal, and Anansi.

   • Animal stories and fables, stories in which animals talk and act like people.

   • Tales of heroes and wonders, for example, "Jack and the Beanstalk," "Cinderella," "The House Between Earth and Sky," and "Hassan and the Island of the Djinn."

3. Ask your elders to talk with you about what these stories meant to them growing up. What did they learn from the stories? Were there lessons about life or special feelings they remember having from special stories?

Conclusion: Process and Products

Once you have done the bulk of your folklore collecting, it is important to have ways to process what you have discovered for the use and enjoyment of the school and the community. One excellent way is to select, edit, and lay out the collection to make a printed book, which can be inexpensively bound and duplicated. A second way is to coach the students in performance and create a storytelling troupe that can share your collection with students in other classes, other grades, and even other schools. A third way is to create a multicultural folk festival, or if such an event already exists at your school, to devise ways to weave the folklore collections and storytelling activities from your residency into the festive mix. All three ways will be great fun, all will benefit the students and the teachers involved, and all will involve a substantial investment of time, energy, and effort. The good news is that you may be so excited by the results that you won't notice just how much work you've put into it.

If you choose to make a book, you will need to form a team of workers willing to help select the best stories from your collection, to edit them for consistency of grammar and style, to type them into a word processor, to arrange them into some visually artful and logical order, and to supervise the printing. You may want to enlist the collaboration of visual art classes to produce illustrations or graphics for the book as well. You will also need to secure signed release forms from the students granting you permission to include their stories (see sample release form at the end of this chapter).

Each of these steps involves delicate labor-management issues. In my experience in the Chicago schools, only somewhere between twenty and thirty percent of stories collected are significant and coherent enough to print. Of that small percentage, many require much editing to make their bare outlines clear and readable. Editing chores can be assumed either by the storytelling specialist, the lead teacher or teachers on the project, or by students working in supervised committees.

If there are ethnic culture clubs already in place in the school, these clubs may be involved in developing material from each group.

Either the teacher, the storytelling specialist, or both must be ultimately responsible for supervising the collation and final arrangement. Having the teacher or the specialist take an active part in the editing process means that there will be an adult who is able to say "No" to incomplete, trivial, or inappropriate material, which can be a political safety valve. You should look for the best balance between tasks that can be given away to eager and able students and tasks that are best kept in experienced hands. But the editors should take pains to be as inclusive as they sensibly can, striving to find that happy medium between inclusiveness, reader-friendliness, and production budget. There is a significant cost difference between a fifty-page booklet and a hundred-and-fifty-page collection. How many total pages can you afford to reproduce in the quantities that your school will need?

Repetitions and story fragments will not help the book in the eyes of readers. Nor will inconsistent grammar and spelling. Though the students must be gentled and encouraged into the collection process, it serves no one to allow them to look awkward in print.

You will need to decide whether to concentrate on folktales, as I do, or to include personal and family narratives, autobiographical tales. These kinds of stories can be riveting, deeply moving, even cathartic. They can also, by the same token, be traumatic. The experiences of immigrants and refugees are a practically unfathomable compound of hope and darkness. In specially constructed workshop environments of well-earned trust, these stories can be a revelation to explore and to share. In more general, mixed classroom environments, traditional tales from the home countries can provide a safe intermediary space as well as powerful educational tools in themselves for all of the reasons already discussed.

You will also need to decide how much to leaven the story collection with recipes, remedies, beliefs, proverbs, and oral history interviews. The famous Foxfire collections have shown how successful such general collections of lore can be. In the absence of a storytelling specialist with particular interest and expertise in the labor-intensive process of selecting and editing stories, the general approach may be more pragmatic. Both kinds of collections are valuable and can produce wonderful results. Your choices will depend on the community at hand, on the materials you receive, and on the personnel you have available to task.

Making a book takes resources. The longer your edited collection is, the greater your costs of production will be. In Chicago I always wrote an estimate of production costs into our grant proposals. We scoured for matching funds and in-kind contributions from local businesses, from school stockpiles, and from other school resources such as computer labs, printing equipment, and staff time. I also volunteered a fair amount of my time to put the booklets together—some of which was compensated by grant funds, some of which was recorded as in-kind contribution, and some of which was entered on the section of the balance sheet headed "Experience."

So may your experiences reading and adapting the exercises and tales in this book be as illuminating and fruitful as mine have been assembling them. Onward to the Ocean of Story!

Folklore Project
Sample Release Form

I, _____, do hereby

grant permission to _____, editor of the

_____ TESOL Folklore Project and its associated

publications, to reprint my contributed story, proverb, remedy, or recipe in a collection of

folklore from the _____Schools. I understand that

individual contributors' percentage of total royalties will be donated by the publishers to

the following nonprofit organizations for the support of education and the arts:

_____

_____

I waive all claim to monetary compensation for this contribution to the project.

_____

Signed

_____

Date

Folklore and Oral History Interviewing Resources

Books

Banks, Ann. *First Person America.* New York: Vintage, 1980.

Botkin, Ben. *Lay My Burden Down: A Folk History of Slavery.* Chicago: University of Chicago Press, 1945.

Brecher, Jeremy. *History from Below: How to Uncover and Tell the Story of Your Community, Association, or Union.* New Haven: CT: Advocate Press, 1986.

Davis, Marilyn. *Mexican Voices/American Dreams: An Oral History of Mexican Immigration to the United States.* New York: Henry Holt, 1990.

Fontana, Bernard. "American Indian Oral History." *History and Theory*, vol. 8, 1987, 366–370.

Garcia, Mario T. "Chicano History: An Oral History Approach." *Journal of San Diego History*, Winter 1977, 46–54.

Ives, Edward D. *The Tape-recorded Interview: A Manual for Field Workers in Folklore and Oral History.* Knoxville: University of Tennessee Press, 1995.

Ritchie, Donald. *Doing Oral History.* New York: Scribners, 1995.

Rogovin, Paula. *Classroom Interviews: A World of Learning.* Chicago: Heinemann, 1998.

Rosenbluth, Vera. *Keeping Family Stories Alive: A Creative Guide to Taping Your Family Life and Lore.* Point Roberts: WA: Hartly and Marks, 1990.

Terkel, Studs. *The Good War: An Oral History of World War II.* New York: Pantheon Books, 1984.

———. *Hard Times: An Oral History of the Great Depression.* New York: Pantheon, 1970.

———. *Race: How Blacks and Whites Think and Feel about the American Obsession.* New York: New Press, 1992.

Wigginton, Elliott. *The Foxfire Book.* New York: Anchor, 1972.

———. *Foxfire,* vols. 2–9. New York: Anchor, 1973–1986.

Web sites

http://www.crt.state.la.us/folklife/edu_unit5ss_folk_trad_intr.html

Introduction to "Swapping Stories," a collection of performance-based folktales from Louisiana communities. Excellent article by Carl Lindahl on story types and on the representational issues involved in going from tape recordings to print.

http://www.crt.state.la.us/folklife/main_prog_storytell_projec.html

Web site for Louisiana State Folklife Program's "Swapping Stories" project. Interesting multimedia presentation of the state's traditional storytelling communities, tradition bearers, and folktale repertoires, in print, video, audio, and Web-based formats.

http://educate.si.edu/migrations/seek1/grand1.html

Instructional Web site for the Smithsonian Institution's folklore collecting model project. Includes pages on interview methods, equipment, rationale, modes of presentation, and an extensive bibliography.

http://lcweb.loc.gov/folklife/fieldwk.html

The folklore fieldwork guide from the American Folklife Center of the Library of Congress. Contains useful basic information on standards of collecting in the folklore field.

http://web.nmsu.edu/~publhist/ohindex.html

Web site of New Mexico State University Public and Community History Program. Includes solid outline of the theory and practical methodology of Oral History, as well as a useful bibliography and links.

PART 2

THE OCEAN OF STORY

There is a ten-volume Sanskrit story collection, the Katha Sarit Sagara *(The Ocean of Story), that was written down in the eleventh century A.D. by a Kashmiri poet named Bhatta Somadeva. According to C. H. Tawney, the English translator of that work, Somadeva "felt that his great work united in itself all stories, as the ocean does all rivers. Every stream of myth and mystery flowing down from the snowy heights of sacred Himalaya would sooner or later reach the ocean; other streams from other mountains would do likewise, till at last fancy would create an ocean full of stories of every conceivable description . . . "*

Though hardly as full as that legendary ocean of old, this section traces a new kind of map for the circulating currents of world folklore. From every inhabited continent on earth we have migrant populations in the Chicago Public Schools. All, except for Australia, have given stories to this project. In the following section we take a storytelling trip around the globe. We start out traveling southward through Latin America and the Caribbean; we cross the Atlantic to Eastern Europe, follow the trade routes into the Middle East and the Arabic lands of North Africa, then descend into sub-Saharan East and West Africa. Finally we sail the Indian Ocean to the Philippines and Southeast Asia; we journey through India and Pakistan, finishing in the lands of Somadeva himself. We have skipped a few places further casts of the net would have brought up more species of tales. I hope that others will take up the challenge and dip into this same great sea.

Each story is separately titled and credited to its country of origin as well as the school in which it was collected, except for a few tales that generally appear in cycles—sequences of stories on a single theme or central character—such as "Buried Treasure," "La Llorona," and a couple of sets of Nasruddin Hodja or Gioha tales. The names of the students or teachers who submitted the stories are given in Notes on the Stories at the end of the book.

LATIN AMERICA

Juan El Huevon

Once upon a time there was a boy named Juan El Huevon—Lazy Juan—who hated to work. All he did was lie around the house all day and scratch himself.

One day his mother said, "Juan! Get up and go find some work and earn your keep!" So Juan got up and went out into the street and the first person he came to he asked her for a job. It so happened that the woman ran a furniture store. She said, "Okay, I'll give you a job in my store."

She took Juan to the store and said, "Clean the whole showroom while I go to town to buy some more goods." She meant for Juan to wash and mop the floor and to polish the furniture. But when she left the store, Juan took all the furniture and threw it out the back door.

When the owner came back and saw what Juan had done, she was furious. "What is all my furniture doing out on the patio?"

Juan said, "You told me to clean the whole room."

"Go home, get out, you're fired."

So Juan went sadly home to his mother. When he told her what had happened, she said, "Well you can't stay here doing nothing. Go and work for the Devil, for all I care. But make sure he pays you in advance."

Juan's mother thought she was making a bitter joke. But Juan didn't get the joke. So he walked out of the house and started up the mountain road, looking for the Devil, to see if he could work for him.

Sure enough, he hadn't gone far before he met a man all dressed in black, with a wide-brimmed sombrero on his head, riding a black horse.

"I hear you're looking for a job," said the Devil.

"Are you the Devil? My mother said I should go to work for you. But you have to pay me in advance."

The Devil reached into his saddlebags and pulled out a bag of gold. "Give this to your mother and come with me," he said.

So Juan ran back to his mother's house and threw her the heavy bag of gold, saying, "Mama, I made the Devil pay us in advance, like you told me to." Then he ran back up the mountain road to where the Devil was waiting. He got on the horse behind the Devil and they rode off to Hell.

When they got to the Devil's house, the Devil turned to Juan and said, "I've got to get back to work, and my eight sons are all at school. This is a good time to wash my dining room table and chairs. Do it." And the Devil left Juan alone in the house.

Well, Juan looked in the Devil's cabinets for soap. He found a white sticky substance and mixed it up with water and poured it all over the Devil's fine old dining room table and chairs. Then he scrubbed and he scrubbed, but he couldn't get the white sticky substance off the table or the chairs. Finally he got tired, so he lay down and went to sleep.

While Juan was sleeping, the Devil's eight sons came home from school. They got out some food and sat down at the table to eat. But when they put their arms on the table they couldn't pick them up again. And when they tried to get up out of their chairs they found they couldn't move. To wash the Devil's fine dining room furniture Juan El Huevon had used glue.

When the Devil came home from work he found his eight sons crying and screaming, with their arms stuck to the table and their backsides stuck to the chairs. The Devil looked around for Juan and found him sleeping peacefully in the corner of the kitchen.

"Get out of here, go home, you're fired!"

So Juan went home to his mother's house. But because he'd been sure to get the Devil to pay him in advance, they had enough money to live on for the rest of their lives. And Juan El Huevon never had to work again.

—Mexico (Pierce)

The Hen of the Quince Hills

Around the town of Zinapecuaro in Michoacan they tell the story of the hen of the Quince Hills and her seven maids.

Long ago in conquistador times there was a people, the Tarazca Indians, who made their dwelling within a hill, a hill that to this day produces many beautiful flowering quince trees. The Tarazca were fearful that the Spanish would take their treasures, so they made a pyramid at the foot of the hill.

In that place there lived a beautiful princess who fell in love with a Spanish captain against the wishes of her people. Her father commanded her not to go near the white men, but she went astray and fell in love with one Captain Hugo Villadiego.

The story goes that as punishment her father locked her inside the pyramid. There she died of grief.

It is said that every year on Good Friday, a hen with seven chicks comes out of the grotto and goes to the pyramid. This is the princess Atzimba and her seven maids. They say that anyone who can trap the hen and her seven chicks will break the spell and will be master of all the treasures that are hidden in the hill. But first he must carry the creatures all the way from the hill to the church in the center of town, so that "Señor Cura," the priest of the church, can give them his blessing.

The story is told that once a poor man ventured out on the holy day and was able to trap the hen with her seven chicks. He caught them in a bag and threw the bag over his shoulder. And then he heard a voice behind him saying, "Take me to the church and don't turn around. Even if they tell you to, don't turn around."

The man carried the bag into town. Everyone he met cried out him, "Stop, look at what you're carrying, don't come any further, throw it away!" Or else they fled from him in terror. But the man kept going, and he didn't turn around. He had to walk about five kilometers from the hill to the church. When he was nearly there, he met a group of women who were running toward him and shouting, "Stop, look what you are carrying on your shoulder!" This time he couldn't stop himself—he turned around and looked. There on his back was an enormous feathered serpent with seven heads.

The man fell dead on the spot from the shock.

The serpent slithered back through the town to the hill of the quince trees. The legend has it that every year on Good Friday you can still see the hen with her seven chicks there. No one has yet taken her as far as the church to be blessed.

—Mexico (Pierce)

You Can't Please Everybody

Once upon a time there was a father and son who wanted to travel from their village to a distant town. They were so poor that all they had for transportation was an old gray donkey.

They left their village early in the morning. The man and his son both perched on the donkey's back and slowly lurched along the road. As they were passing through a village called San Luis, they heard the townspeople talking about them. "What a cruel family—they're both perfectly happy on top of that poor beast, but what about the donkey? They'll kill him, riding two at a time like that."

The father and son felt ashamed of themselves. Quickly they both climbed down from the donkey's back and continued their journey on foot, side-by-side with their donkey. As they passed through a town called La Paz, they heard the people talking about them again. "What a pair of idiots—they both walk when they could be riding. The donkey must be laughing at them!"

Shame-faced, the man pushed his son up onto the donkey's back, and they traveled that way for some time. As they passed through the town of San Juan, they heard the people talking about them again. "Look at that boy—sitting pretty while his poor father scrapes along behind. Has he no respect for his elders?"

Shame-faced, the boy jumped down and gave his seat to his father, and they went on. When they came to the last village before their destination, they heard the people talking again. "What kind of father is that, riding happily along while his poor little boy struggles along on foot?"

At this they stopped. The father turned to his son and said, "We can't win. We'll never please everyone in every town. We'll just have to do what we like best, because all these opinions are making donkeys of us both." So they both got up on the donkey's back, and on they went on to their destination.

—Mexico (Roosevelt)

The Water of Life

Once upon a time there was a very poor man who lived with his wife and so many children that they could hardly keep food on the table. The man was used to going hungry so that his children could have enough to eat. But one day he reached the end of his endurance. "All I want," he said to his wife, "is a chicken—one whole chicken that I can eat by myself. But I don't expect to see such a thing in this life."

His wife, however, was a resourceful woman who took pity on her husband. "I'll take in washing from other people, and with the extra money," she said, "I'll buy you a chicken and cook it so that you can eat by yourself." So she did, and she gave the whole chicken to her husband and told him to go to the woods by himself and eat it.

The man walked deep in the forest till he came to a sandy beach. There he sat down under a tree to eat his chicken. But just as he raised the first morsel to his lips, the Devil appeared in his broad-brimmed hat. "Will you give me a bite of your chicken?" the Devil asked.

"No," said the man. "You're the Devil and you have all the power in the world. But what do you ever give to the poor?" The Devil disappeared in a puff of smoke.

But before the man could take his first bite, an old man with a long white beard appeared before him. It was God. "Would you share a bite of your chicken with me?" God asked.

"No," said the man. "You're the Lord of Heaven and Earth and you can move mountains if you want too, and all you have to say about the poor is that they'll always be here. Well then, go mooch off somebody else's chicken." And God disappeared.

He was about to take that first bite when a skeleton appeared before him, quiet and dignified as a tomb. It was Señor Muerte—Death himself.

"Well," said the man, "don't you look thin and hungry. I suppose you want a bite of my chicken too?"

Death nodded.

"You know what?" said the man. "I think I'm going to share my meal with you. You don't care whether a body is rich or poor—you take 'em just the same. You like white meat or dark?"

Death shrugged.

"All the same to you, eh?" said the man. "Well, sit down and take a load off your bones." And they ate.

When bones were all that were left of that whole cooked chicken, the skeleton stood up, belched, and said to the man, "Thank you. That was excellent. My compliments to your wife. Now, since you saw fit to share your meal with me, I'm going to make you a powerful man."

Death produced a gallon jug and told the man to fill it with water and sand. When this was done, Death shook the jug and blessed it, and said, "This is the water of life. With this you can free both rich and the poor from my grasp." And Death disappeared.

The man took the gallon jug home with him. When he got there he found that one of his sons had been bitten by a poisonous snake and was fighting for his life. But one swallow of water from the jug and Death released his grip.

From then on, the man went up and down the world curing rich and poor alike. From the poor he took no fees, but from the rich he took all he could, until he and his family were as rich as any, and he could afford to eat whole chickens every night.

But when he had taken the last swallow from his jug of the water of life, then Death came for him, too, and wrapped him in its bony arms and never asked if he was rich or poor.

—Mexico (Roosevelt)

Three Pieces of Advice

Once upon a time in Mexico there was a very poor man who had to leave his wife and his young son to go and look for work. For many years he wandered from town to town, doing odd jobs and trying his best to earn a few pesos.

One day, on the road to yet another town, he met a little old man. The old man had a long white beard, and the wisdom of the ages in his face. They hailed each other and stopped to talk. "You look like a man of some experience," said the poor man to the old one. "Maybe you could give me some advice, to help me with my problems."

"Sure," said the old man. "It's more blessed to give than to receive. So if you'll take my advice I'd gladly give it.

"First, don't leave the main road for a shortcut.

"Second, don't ask questions about things that don't concern you.

"And third, don't take action without considering the consequences."

The poor man thanked the little old man and continued on his way.

The next day the man met a group of travelers who were going to the same town as he. They walked the road together for a while, till they came to a fork in the road. One of the other travelers said that the little footpath was a shortcut, and all the rest of them wanted to take it. But our hero remembered the old man's first piece of advice: Don't leave the main road for a shortcut. So he let his companions go by the footpath while he continued on the main road.

When he got to town, the news had just arrived that a party of travelers had been attacked by bandits on the trail nearby, and all of them had been killed. The poor man silently thanked the old one for saving his life.

Sometime after that, he came to a prosperous little *ranchito*. The owner made him welcome and gave him work and room and board. The next day, when the man met the owner's wife, he noticed that she was very frail and looked terribly unhappy. He wanted to ask her why, but he remembered the old man's second piece of advice: Don't ask questions about things that don't concern you. So he held his tongue.

Because of this, the owner of the *ranchito* came to trust him, and soon he was managing the entire estate. In the course of time the owner and his wife passed away and left the man the *ranchito* and a small fortune along with it.

Finally the man decided that it was time to go home and see his wife and his son. More than twelve years had passed since he went away. When he reached his old house, he looked in the bedroom window, and there on the bed asleep he saw a stranger.

My wife is living with another man, he thought, and instinctively he reached for his knife. But suddenly it flashed upon his mind the old man's third piece of advice: Don't take action without considering the consequences. So he simply went to the door and knocked.

His wife was overjoyed to see him, and she called for their son. Out of the bedroom came the same young man he had seen through the window, now grown to adulthood.

The next day the three of them set off for the *ranchito* where the husband was now the *padrone*. On the way, the father said to his son, "Always listen to the advice of the wise. It can bring you prosperity and happiness, and it can even save your life."

—Mexico (Senn)

El Sombreron

A long time ago in Tula Hidalgo, it was said that the oil refinery was built through a pact between the owner and the Devil, who was known to the people by the name of El Sombreron, because he always appeared to them in a wide-brimmed sombrero.

The owner of the refinery project had everything, men and supplies, all ready to begin construction. But when the men came to work each morning, they would find all that they had done the day before had been undone in the night. They couldn't explain how this had happened, but it happened just the same way for a week. Finally, one morning as the men were clearing the debris from the previous day's ruined work, a man appeared dressed like a *charro* (a Mexican cowboy), wearing an enormous wide-brimmed hat. It was El Sombreron. "You boys are wasting your time," he told them. "I'm not letting you build anything until I have a pact with the owner of this land." Then he disappeared.

The construction workers were terrified and ran to tell the owner. He didn't believe them. But the work kept getting ruined each night. One night the owner decided to stay at the construction site and watch. At midnight, El Sombreron appeared and told the owner that he wanted to make a deal with him. If the deal were made, then El Sombreron would let the construction proceed.

"What do you want from me?" asked the owner.

El Sombreron said that he wanted the souls of children from the locality, starting right away—and of old people too, but not for a while.

The owner said that he had no objection to anything El Sombreron wanted to take from the local people, just as long as he could build his refinery on his land.

Soon after that, children began to disappear from the local towns and villages, never to be seen again. But construction on the refinery proceeded without any hindrance. Two years later it was completed. The owner became fabulously wealthy.

After a few years, El Sombreron appeared again to the refinery owner. He said it was time to collect on the second part of their agreement. He had had his fill of children; now he wanted the souls of older people. The owner said that he had given his word—El Sombreron could have what he wanted.

Days later there was a terrible explosion at the refinery. Many workers at the plant were killed, and toxic smoke from the blast killed many older people in the town whose lungs were already weakened by years of breathing the refinery fumes.

People said that it was all because of the pact between the owner and El Sombreron.

—Mexico (Roosevelt)

What the Dogs Saw

Not long ago in the Mexican state of Guerrero, there lived an old woman named Rosa who was always getting into other people's business. She lived in a little house with a donkey, some hens, a rooster, and a pack of squinty-eyed dogs, across a dry *arroyo* from the churchyard. This old woman used to wonder about everything under the sun, and she carried whatever news she could get ahold of to wherever she had no business carrying it.

But one thing she never could find out was why her pack of squinty-eyed dogs took to howling every night when the church bell struck midnight. She would yell at them to stop, beat them with a broom handle, curse them with oaths that would shame the Devil—but they wouldn't stop howling till they were ready, a good hour or two after they'd begun. In the morning Rosa would take her favorite mutt, Maria, under the chin and pull her nose about, saying, "What were you howling at last night, Maria, you braying jackass?" But Maria just squinted and squirmed and never answered a Christian word.

Rosa asked the question of everyone she knew in town, but if anyone knew what the dogs were howling at, they weren't telling Rosa. The most she got out of anyone was from the priest, who said sternly, "That is something you'd be better off not to be asking."

But Rosa remembered a bit of wisdom her grandmother used to tell when Rosa was just a little girl: "If you want to see what the dogs see at night, rub a little sleep from the corner of one of their eyes into your own eye, and look."

So one night Rosa grabbed Maria by the nose, and she picked a little sleep out of the corner of the dog's eye, rubbed it in her own two eyes, and looked out toward the arroyo. And there she saw what the dogs saw.

Coming across the arroyo from the churchyard was a line of ghostly figures moving in a slow, stately procession along the dry creek bed at the edge of her yard. Some wore white robes, others dark shrouds, and still others were nothing but skeletons and wore nothing but their bones. Each figure held a tall white candle before it, which gave a pale, eerie glow to the procession. On and on they came, the hosts of the dead, and Rosa's pack of squinty-eyed dogs howled after them as if maddened by the sight, and nothing but death itself could have stopped their howls.

Rosa stood still, unblinking and barely breathing, all the while the ghosts were going by. In the midst of this gruesome parade, the howling of her dogs receded for her into a kind of a soft background music. If every muscle in her body hadn't been frozen, she might have howled herself. Finally there came a dark-robed figure who brought up the very end of the line; but before he disappeared into the madrone thicket where the arroyo met the corner of her land, he turned to Rosa, and extended his long bony arm in her direction. All the way up from the arroyo his arm floated to her, offering her his tall white candle. She didn't want to take it, but she was afraid that it would fall and burn up her whole property. So she grabbed it, and when she did, the night was black again and the dogs were whimpering and slinking away to their sleeping spots.

The candle too was dark, and Rosa thought the ghost must have blown it out when it handed it to her. But when she took it inside and lit the lamp, she saw that it was the long bone of an arm. She gave a scream and threw the bone out the door as far as she could into the night. But when she got up in the morning, the bone was lying in the corner of her house.

She boxed Maria's ears and threw the bone deep into the arroyo. Next morning there it was again, in the corner of the house. The dogs were milling around outside looking innocent and hungry. Rosa realized that this was something beyond their control or hers.

So she went to the priest. He told her that she would have to stand outside with the bone candle tonight and watch for the last ghost of the procession to pass her house—saying her rosary all the while—and she should give him back the bone candle that he had given her. And then the whole procession would vanish from her sight and she would never more be troubled with it—if she never again wiped the sleep from the corners of her dogs' eyes and stopped asking into things that were none of her business.

So she did. The ghostly procession vanished, and Rosa was never troubled with it again. And she never wiped the sleep from the corner of her dogs' eyes, and she stopped asking into things that were none of her business.

—Mexico (Roosevelt)

The Black Cat Ate His Soul

This is a story that the old people in Mexico tell to the children. Once upon a time there was a boy who never listened to his parents, and he always went to bed angry. One day, when his school gave out report cards, his parents found out that he had failed some classes. His parents were nagging him about it, but he only got angry, as usual, and he went to his room and locked himself in for the rest of the day. His parents were sorry, but not surprised.

The sun went down and the boy got hungry and thirsty. But he wouldn't come out of his room, because then he would have to face his parents. So he went to sleep, still hungry and thirsty and angry.

While he was sleeping, his soul left his body and went to the well to get some water because it was parched with thirst and weak with anger. A black cat was out hunting in the night and saw the boy's soul, and because the soul was hungry and thirsty and angry and all alone, the cat was able to catch it and eat it. So the boy never woke up. He died in his sleep, because the cat ate his soul.

That's why some people in my country say that it is bad to go to sleep hungry, or thirsty, or angry at someone. Because it may set the soul on a dangerous path. And we never know when we lie down at night whether we will rise up the next day or not.

—Mexico (Roosevelt)

The Horseman in the Whirlwind

In Mexico they say that there was once a beautiful girl who loved to go to dances and to dance with every man who asked her. There were many who wanted to marry her and settle down, but she was light-hearted and light on her feet, and no man was good enough for her to marry—but every man was good enough for a dance.

But one night in the middle of the dancing a handsome stranger appeared to her. He was the handsomest man she had ever seen, tall and dark and dressed in the costume of a wealthy caballero. She came toward him, he took her in his arms, and they began to dance, whirling faster and faster and faster—until he suddenly turned into a whirlwind and swept her up out of the dance hall and into the air. The whirlwind finally set her down in the branches of a nagual cactus, torn and bleeding.

Early in the morning she was found and rescued and healed of her wounds—but in her heart she was still torn and fearful. One day she was going for water at the river when the caballero appeared to her again. She was so frightened that she ran home and told her parents, but they didn't believe her, which made her all the more afraid. So she went to the priest and made confession. He was the only one to believe her. The priest told her that if this horseman should appear to her again, she should not be afraid, just ask him what it was he wanted from her.

Later that day the girl was home alone, and she looked up and saw the horseman standing close beside her. She was not afraid, she just stood her ground and asked, "What do you want from me?"

The horseman replied, "Your life."

She broke away from him and ran back to the church. No one was there. But she knelt alone by the altar and prayed to God with all her heart. All night she knelt and prayed there, and then she walked out into the morning light. The horseman never appeared to her again, and she lived in peace for the rest of her days.

—Mexico (Roosevelt)

The Snake Husband

Long ago in Yucatan there lived a widower and his daughter. In the course of time, the widower married another woman who had no feelings for her stepdaughter. The girl spent most of her time by herself, wandering the jungle and the seashore. She grew up half wild.

One day when the girl was off by herself in the jungle, she met a handsome young man. He talked to her and he was kind, although there was something strange about him, too. But this didn't bother her—she felt they were two of a kind.

They met again and again, and soon they became intimate. After a while, the girl's belly began to swell, but she kept it a secret. The stepmother suspected something was up, but she couldn't tell what.

Then one morning the girl stayed in her room. She didn't go out all day, nor the next, nor the next. After three days the girl came out of her room. She went quickly through the house without speaking to her father or her stepmother, and she went off to the jungle like she used to do.

When she had gone, the stepmother went into the girl's room to look around. In the course of poking into this drawer and that, she happened to open up the chest that was at the foot of the girl's bed. It was full of little baby snakes.

"*Ayeeee!*" The stepmother ran out of the room to tell her husband—without shutting the lid of the chest. And some of the baby snakes crawled out of the chest and wriggled away, never to return.

When the girl came home that night she went straight to her room without saying a word to anyone. But a moment later she came rushing out again, so angry that her face was twisted. In the bosom of her dress were all the little baby snakes that were left inside the chest. They were crawling on her shoulders and in her hair. The girl never spoke to her father or her stepmother. Instead she left the house, and went far, far away, to a cave on a mountainside, overlooking the ocean, that was called the Cave of the Sea. And there she stayed, with her husband and their children.

Her father missed her and grieved for her. One day he went to the Cave of the Sea, hoping to meet her. He found her there, and with much sadness he asked, "Daughter, what are you doing here? Why did you leave us this way?"

"It's not your fault, father," she told him. "That woman, my stepmother, she doesn't care for me, and she doesn't want my children. That's why I'm living here now. But I will come back to visit you, and I will bring my husband."

"We didn't even know that you got married," her father said.

"My husband is part human and part snake," she said. "His name is Rey. This is his home."

She was silent for a moment, and then she said, "You must go now. But we will come and visit soon. And when we do, I want you to have put five empty boxes on the front porch. And don't be afraid when you see my husband."

Her father went home, got the boxes, and left them on the porch. That night, he and the stepmother were awakened by strange, loud noises. They looked out the window and they saw their daughter walking beside a gigantic snake. The strange noises were the sound of his hissing and the sound of his thick body sliding over the ground. As they watched, the snake began to shed his skin, and out stepped a handsome man. When he appeared, the boxes on the porch began to fill with gold.

When the boxes were full to the brim, the man stepped back into his snakeskin, and he became the gigantic snake again. The daughter took one last look at her father's house. Then they turned and went back to their home in the Cave of the Sea.

They lived a happy life up there, people say. The father didn't see much of his daughter after that. But if he needed to, he knew where to find her.

—Mexico (Mather)

In Latin America, there are many legends of buried treasure. Here are a few of them.

Buried Treasure

Once upon a time there was a village where there lived a good-hearted farmer. Everybody in town knew this farmer because he was kind and helpful to everyone he met. This farmer had a wife and a daughter, and he also had a neighbor by the name of Alfonzo.

One day the good-hearted farmer's daughter got sick. He wanted to stay home from work and take care of her, but his wife told him that he had to go to the fields to sow because they needed the money to take the daughter to the doctor. If he stayed home the whole day, they would have no money for medicine, and the girl could die.

So the farmer went to the fields, with his heart full of worry for his child. But as he was sowing his corn, he noticed an incandescent light coming from a little hill nearby. He paid it little mind, being preoccupied with his work and with thoughts of his daughter.

When it was nearly dark, the farmer started back to his house, but on his way he stopped to visit his friend Alfonzo. He wanted to see if Alfonzo could lend him some money to take his child to the doctor. Alfonzo said that he had no money. But as they were talking, the farmer happened to mention the incandescent light he had seen coming from the ground. Alfonzo remembered something that he had heard about these lights from the ground—that they meant that there was treasure buried underneath. The farmer saw a far-off look come into Alfonzo's face, and he asked him, "What are you thinking?"

Alfonzo told him, "Nothing." They continued talking for a little. Then Alfonzo asked again about the light—where it was exactly. The farmer told him. Alfonzo said nothing more about it, but when the farmer had gone he hurried to that place with a pick and shovel to try and find the gold and precious stones that he knew would be buried there. When he reached the place he began to dig furiously—but all he found was a great lump of coal.

"Coal? Coal! What do I want with coal?" Alfonzo exclaimed. But suddenly he remembered something else that he had heard about the lights—that anyone who follows one of those light out of greed for gold or gain would never receive any good of it. Sorrowfully, Alfonzo buried the lump of coal where he had found it and went home.

The next day, the good-hearted farmer went to the fields again, thinking only of his work and of his daughter. As he went along turning over the earth with his mattock, he happened to come to the little hill where yesterday he had seen the incandescent light. Still thinking only of his work, he turned over the soil in that place, and under his mattock he saw gold and precious stones in the place where his friend had found coal.

The good-hearted farmer took the treasure he had found and changed it for money. First he and his wife took their daughter to the doctor and bought medicines that made her well. Then, they used their money to help the poor people in the town to buy homes and food.

When he came to his friend Alfonzo's house, Alfonzo was ashamed. "There is something I must tell you," Alfonzo said. And he confessed that he had gone to dig at the place himself, but because of his greed he had only found a lump of coal. "But you, because of your good heart, you found what was there to find."

The good-hearted farmer forgave Alfonzo for what he had done, and he even gave him some money to build a new house. And in that way all the people of the village benefited from one man's good fortune.

—Mexico (Roosevelt)

Gold or Charcoal?

Once there was a man who loved to hunt for buried treasure. He had heard about money buried at a certain place, but when he arrived at the place and began to dig, all he found was a pot full of charcoal. He took it to his house and put some of the charcoal pieces in a bottle. The rest he saved in the attic of his house.

One day his *compadre* came and saw the bottle of charcoal, and he asked the man how he had fit the gold coins in the mouth of the bottle.

"No, *compadre*—there's no gold coins in that bottle, it's only charcoal."

"No, *compadre*—you have gold coins in the bottle."

"*Compadre*—do you see coins in the bottle?"

"Yes, *compadre,* I see gold coins."

"Then I have something else to show you." He took his *compadre* to the attic and showed him the pot full of charcoal.

"*Compadre*—where did you get all this gold?"

"*Compadre*—do you see gold?"

"Yes *compadre*—look." And he emptied the pot of charcoal onto the floor, and then the man saw that it was really gold.

—Mexico (Roosevelt)

Pesos

This is a story that happened in the Mexican state of Michoacan, in a little village called Sabaneta. In Sabaneta there lived an old man who had a lot of money. The villagers called the old man "Pesos." Whenever anyone in the village needed money they would go to Pesos, and he would lend them money at high rates of interest. No one knew where Pesos got his money. But one day a villager named Pancho decided that he would find out.

So he followed Pesos when he went out into the countryside. Pancho watched as Pesos came to a great rock. He saw Pesos take off all his clothes and tie a moneybag around his waist. Then he saw Pesos get down on all fours and snort and paw the ground like a bull. Pesos charged at the rock and rammed it head-first, and the next thing Pancho knew, Pesos had disappeared into the rock.

Pancho didn't know what to make of this; but he sat still and watched. After a while he saw Pesos charge out of the rock into the daylight, and now the bag around his waist was full of gold coins.

Pesos put his clothes back on and went home with his bag of gold. Now Pancho was alone. He thought about what he had seen. It didn't look easy. But Pancho thought, I'm as tough as that old man. So he got down in front of the rock, took off all his clothes, made a bag out of his serape, and tied it around his waist. Then Pancho got down on all fours, pawed the ground, and snorted like a bull, and he charged head-first at the rock.

Bam! He was in a cave, and there was gold all around, more gold than he could ever carry home. He filled his serape with the gold and tied it back around his waist. But when he looked for an opening in the rock, he couldn't find any. Everything in the cave looked different. Pancho grew confused and afraid, and when he got down on all fours and rammed the wall, he almost broke his skull.

Terrified and in great pain, Pancho threw down the serape full of gold, and when he did, he found himself outside the rock, with all his clothes (except for his serape) scattered around him on the ground.

Pancho went home with nothing but a lump on his head and a missing serape for his troubles. He said that only Pesos knew how to get into the rock *and* how to get out. And he never did find out how Pesos did it.

—Mexico (Roosevelt)

The Blue Light

In Peru there's a story that goes like this: In a small village near Lima called El Cuzco, there was a very poor man. He hardly had anything to eat or any clothes to wear.

He lived in a small house near the mountains. One night he was outside smoking a cigarette; suddenly he saw a blue light at the top of the mountain. He was very surprised. After a moment he decided to follow the trail till he reached the blue light. It was around midnight already. It took him hours, but he finally reached the light, and he threw his coat over it and lay down next to it to sleep.

When he awoke in the first morning light, the first thing he wanted to do was see if that light was still there. So he lifted up his coat, and beneath it he saw great big gold coins. He couldn't believe his luck. He cried and gave thanks to God for what had happened to him. After that he became the richest person in the village.

Some people say that the Incas had left great stores of gold hidden in different places all over Peru, guarded by these blue lights. Anyway, if you ever go there and see a blue light on top of a mountain, you know what to do.

—Peru (Roosevelt)

Probably the best known folk legend of the Hispanic world is the legend of La Llorona, the Weeping Woman. As with any legend, the details change from telling to telling. Here are a few of the variations. Some tellings may have mingled in details from the case of Susan Smith, the South Carolina mother who killed her own children in 1994—an interesting example of a folk tradition absorbing what crosses its path.

La Llorona

In colonial days, in the age of the Spanish Inquisition, there was a young girl by the name of Ines. She fell in love with a handsome Spanish soldier and had three children with him without being married. He always promised that he would marry her—he even gave her a ring as a sign of his love. But whenever his superiors ordered him to go somewhere else, he went, and he had other girls in other towns to whom he made the same empty promises.

She knew that her lover adored their three children, so to take her revenge on him she killed them, all three, and threw their bodies in the river. The Inquisition condemned her to burn at the stake for her crime. Before she died they told her that she would never be pardoned by God until she brought Him the souls of the three lost children. So ever since that time she has wandered the rivers of Mexico, crying, "*O, mis hijos! O, mis hijos!*—O my children, O my children!" Her voice can still be heard along the rivers and the canyons. Some say it's the wind. Others say it's La Llorona.

—Mexico (Roosevelt)

This story started in the colonial age. They say that there was a beautiful, rich woman who loved her husband. But one day she saw her husband with another woman. She was very angry with her husband and she thought that the way to take revenge on him was to kill her three children by drowning them in a river. She was out of her mind with jealousy. So she took her three children to the river and threw them in and they drowned.

She came back home like nothing had happened. When her husband came home he asked for his sons, and she said, "I thought they were with you." So they went out searching for the children. All night long they searched, but they didn't find them because they were in the river, and she didn't tell him. After two more days she broke down and told her husband what she had done. She said, "I did it because I saw you with another woman and I didn't know what I was doing."

"That woman you saw was my cousin," he said. "She came to visit us."

When the woman heard that, she went crazy. Her husband left her and she went to the river crying, "*Hay mis hijos, hay mis hijos,*" which means, "Where are my sons?" They say that she died but that her soul is still there around the rivers in Mexico, and that she has no rest. Some people say that they have heard her soul screaming there around the rivers, and that her soul will never have rest.

—Mexico (Roosevelt)

Once there was a very happy family: a husband, wife, and their two sons. But one day a friend told Christina, the wife, that her husband was cheating on her. She wanted to make sure, so she went to the bar in town, where she saw her husband, drunk, with another woman. She almost lost her reason. She went home to her twin sons and beat them until she was tired, and then after beating them she threw them in the river alive and they drowned. Soon all the province knew about it, and they burned her alive.

When Christina's soul went before God, He told her that she had been good until the moment she killed her sons. If she could bring to God her sons' lost souls, she would be allowed to enter Heaven.

That's why Christina is always walking by rivers, crying, "*O, mis hijos*—O my sons." And that's why people call her "La Llorona." It's said that this lady appears to drunken men, to scare them away from drinking and from cheating on their wives. But she also appears to children, and if they're not careful, she'll snatch them up and take them to God, to pay Him for the two children she lost.

—Mexico (Roosevelt)

There was a woman who fell in love with a Spanish man. But she had three kids, and she wanted him to think that she was single. So she went to the river and drowned her kids so he would think she was single. But the man didn't want her anyway.

So then she felt bad because she had drowned her kids, and she would cry every day for her kids, till finally she drowned herself.

And people say that they can still hear her crying at night for her kids. Not only by the river, but also in the capitol of Mexico. The meaning of the story is: Never leave or hurt your kids for a man.

—Puerto Rico (Roosevelt)

A girl was in love with a rich man. The guy just wanted sex, but she was really in love with him. She was poor, but she was pretty. She asked the rich guy if he would like to marry her, but he said no. He told her he didn't like weddings. So they had sex without getting married, and she had two boys.

When she told him that she had two boys with him, he told her that he wanted to keep them. But she said that she wanted to get married first. The guy told her that he didn't love her, that he loved another girl who was prettier and wealthier than she was.

So the guy married the other girl and asked the Llorona to give him the boys. But she said no. Her revenge would be to kill the two boys in the river. So she did it.

Five months later she died, and when she went to Hell the Devil told her that her punishment would be to find the boys. So her spirit is in the world, and she goes crying and screaming and looking for her sons in every river of this world.

—Mexico (Roosevelt)

Some people tell of meetings with the spirit of La Llorona. Here is an example:

My uncle tells me that when he was a little kid, one day his father ordered him to go and cut some firewood up in the hills, him and his brothers. My uncle told his brothers to wait for him. When he went to find some firewood the Llorona appeared, and my uncle started running away. The Llorona followed him and cried that he should go with her, because she was his mother. But my uncle didn't listen to her, and he and his brothers ran away.

—Mexico (Roosevelt)

Here is a story that at first glance seems to be a simple tale of witchcraft—but in the end it turns into yet another encounter with La Llorona.

My grandmother was living in a small, quiet village. One day a baby was found dead in a strange way. It was found without blood on its body, but with two tiny holes in its fingers. The people thought that a snake had bitten him. But one month later, another baby was found dead in the same way.

The people began to be afraid, and now no one would leave their babies alone. One night, though, my uncle went to the store to buy cigarettes, and he left the baby alone just for a few minutes. But he forgot his money and had to come back. As he got near, he saw a little light floating through the house; he ran inside, and he saw a woman by the baby's bed. He picked up a stone and he threw it at the woman, and the woman turned and the light was coming from her. She made a jump for the open window and was gone. But my uncle followed the light and he saw it go into an old abandoned house.

He went and told the villagers about it. And the next day the people went and burned down that old house. And when they did, they heard a woman's voice wailing and crying. And to this day, if you pass that house at night, you will probably hear that woman wailing.

—Mexico (Pierce)

I often wondered why the story of La Llorona, of all the legends of Latin America, should be so widely known. Then I heard another version, from Roosevelt's principal, Rafael Sanchez, which gave me a clue. Mr. Sanchez told me that as he had heard the story, it concerned an Indian woman from one of the subjugated tribes of the Aztec empire immediately preceding the Spanish conquest. This woman was taken by the army of the conquistador Hernando Cortez on his march to the Aztec capitol. She became Cortez's concubine and also his translator, helping him negotiate with her own and other conquered tribes, and so to undermine the Aztecs and hasten their collapse. Cortez gave her the Christian name of Maria (or Marina), but to the people she became known as La Malinche (The Tongue).

La Malinche had three children by Cortez. He promised her that when he was done with his conquests he would take her back with him to Spain and marry her. But he had no such intention, and when his mission was completed he returned to his country and to his wife, leaving La Malinche behind.

It was then that an enraged La Malinche drowned the three children that she had borne to Cortez, throwing them in a river, and throwing herself in after. And it is La Malinche, the betrayer of her people and her land, outraged mother of a mixed race and a conquered continent, whose voice haunts the rivers and the arroyos down to this day, crying for her murdered children.

The Fairy Falin

Once upon a time there was a widow with two daughters. The older daughter was ugly, conceited, and very bad-tempered. The younger one, named Alice, was beautiful, sweet, and kind. The mother adored her older daughter and despised the younger. She made Alice do all the work around the house without any rest, and she would only feed her kitchen scraps.

Alice had to go twice a day to fetch water from the water fountain half a league from the house, and she would come home bent double from the weight of the jar. One day, Alice was at the fountain filling the jar when a little old lady approached and asked if she could please have a sip of water from the fountain. Alice kindly gave the woman some of her water.

The old lady told her, "For being so kind, I'll grant you a gift: that every word out of your mouth will turn into a flower, a pearl, or a precious stone."

Poor Alice didn't know what to think—not knowing that this was the fairy Falin, who had turned herself into an old woman to test Alice's goodness. But it was getting late, she didn't know what questions to ask, so she only thanked the old woman and hurried home.

When she got home she was afraid of her mother's anger. "Forgive me mother," she said, "for delaying so much."

As she said these words, two roses, two pearls, and three diamonds fell out of her mouth.

"What am I seeing?" said the mother, stunned. "Daughter, how did this happen?" It was the first time she had called Alice "Daughter."

Alice explained what had happened at the well. The mother immediately decided to send her elder daughter to the well with a silver jar, thinking that this way she would obtain more and better gifts from the old woman.

Casilda, the elder daughter, was so nasty and conceited that she didn't want to go. But the mother convinced her that she wasn't really going for water, but for pearls and precious stones and who knew what else? So away went Casilda with the silver jar, grumbling all the way.

When she reached the fountain, there she met not a little old lady, but a beautiful woman, the fairy Falin in her true guise, who asked for a drink of her water.

Casilda was not impressed. "C'mon!" she said. "Do you think I came all the way over here just to serve you? Let your servants do it!"

"Alright," said Falin, "And since you are so lacking in grace, my gift to you is this: from now on every word from your mouth will turn into a snake, a toad, or a worm."

"What did you get, my precious daughter?" asked the mother when Casilda got home.

"I don't know," said Casilda. But her words dropped from her mouth in the shape of a snake, a toad, and a worm.

"What am I seeing?" cried the mother. "This is surely Alice's fault. But we'll take revenge by killing her right now."

Filled with rage, they went looking for Alice. But Alice had heard their talk, and she fled the house to hide in the forest.

The next day the king's son was in the forest hunting when he came upon a beautiful girl weeping. He stopped and asked why she was so sad. Alice told the prince that her own mother and sister wanted to kill her, and so she had run away. The prince was a good listener, and Alice was desperate for someone to talk to, and soon the clearing was full of pearls, precious stones, and sweet-smelling flowers, dropped from her lips. The prince was much astonished at this girl, whose gifts seemed only a reflection of her goodness of heart. He took her to the palace to meet

58   **Part 2: The Ocean of Story**

his father the king, and it didn't take long to determine that she would make an excellent royal wife.

Meanwhile, as for the mother and Casilda, they lived out their lives surrounded by snakes, toads, and worms, a fitting reward for their cruelty and greed.

—Guatemala (Roosevelt)

Don Coyote and Don Conejo

Once upon a time all the animals lived in peace in one village—until one day the animals began to notice that someone was coming at night and stealing their milk and cheese. Everyone suspected that Don Coyote was to blame. But Don Coyote was very good at stealing, and no one could produce any proof.

Till one day Don Conejo—Rabbit—came up with a plan. He went to Don Coyote and told him that down at the bottom of the lake there was the biggest wheel of white cheese he had ever seen in his life.

Don Coyote's mouth began to water. "Don Conejo, my friend, will you show me this great wheel of cheese?"

"Certainly, friend," said Don Conejo. "Just meet me at the lake shore tonight at midnight."

That night, there was Don Coyote, down by the lake well before midnight, hoping to beat Don Conejo to the cheese. But Don Conejo had figured that Don Coyote would be early, so he was watching from the bushes when Don Coyote first set his eyes on the reflection of the full moon in the still water.

"*Aiiieeee,* mother of God!" cried Coyote, "What a heavenly cheese!" He was so excited that he dove straight into the water and paddled for the bottom. But when he got to the bottom he found no cheese.

Don Coyote spun around and saw the moon shining overhead through the clear water. Then he realized two things at once. First, he realized that he had been tricked by Don Conejo. And second, he realized that he didn't know how to swim. Don Coyote panicked. He swallowed a great big bellyful of water and drowned.

From that time on, all the animals lived in peace once again, without Don Coyote in their midst to steal their milk and cheese.

—Ecuador (Roosevelt)

Juan Bobo's Pig

One day Juan Bobo's mother said to him, "Juanito *mijo,* go and clean up the pig and make her look as beautiful as you can, so that when you take her to market this morning to sell her she will fetch a good price."

Well, Juan Bobo always tried to do exactly as his mother told him. So he went and washed the pig with buckets of soapy water and scrubbed her face with a washcloth—but she still didn't look very beautiful. So Juan Bobo went to his mother's closet and got out her red taffeta skirt with the elastic waistband, and he slipped that around the pig's waist. Then he went to the house of his great-aunt Margarita, who weighed almost three hundred pounds, and he borrowed a blouse and a bright red wig, and he fit those onto the pig. He outlined the pig's eyes as best he could with black eyeliner and a touch of blue eye shadow; he put bright red lipstick on the pig's lips; and he got two pairs of his mother's high heeled pumps and strapped those onto her trotters, and now the pig really did look beautiful. So he put a rope around her neck and started to take her to market.

But halfway along the road to town they came upon a big muddy puddle. This looked really beautiful to the pig. So she threw herself down in the mud and rolled around a couple times, and there was nothing Juan Bobo could do about it—because she was much bigger than he was, and sometimes she just forgot that Juan Bobo was supposed to be in charge. She got the red taffeta skirt all covered with mud, ripped one sleeve out of the blouse, tore off her wig, and completely ruined her mascara.

By the time Juan Bobo got her out of the puddle and all the way to town, she didn't look so beautiful anymore. In fact, the townspeople laughed Juan Bobo and his pig all the way back home. So that today, in Puerto Rico, whenever anyone gets so dressed up that his or her friends almost— but not quite—don't recognize them, people say that person is "dressed up like Juan Bobo's pig."

—Puerto Rico (Roosevelt)

EASTERN EUROPE

Chicken's Great Adventure

Chicken was on her way to the bazaar when she stepped in a puddle of mud right up to her belly.

She went to Bush and said, "Bush, clean my leg."

Bush said, "No."

"Just wait," she said. "I'll get Goat to eat you."

So she went to Goat and said, "Goat, eat Bush, so he'll clean my leg."

Goat said, "No."

"Just wait. I'll get Wolf to bite you."

She went to Wolf and said, "Wolf, bite Goat, so he'll eat Bush, so he'll clean my leg."

Wolf said, "No."

"Just wait. I'll get the Village and it'll beat you."

She went to the Village and said, "Village, beat Wolf, so he'll bite Goat, so he'll eat Bush, so he'll clean my leg."

The Village said, "No."

"Just wait. I'll get Fire and she'll burn you."

She went to Fire and said, "Fire, burn the Village, so it'll beat Wolf, so he'll bite Goat, so he'll eat Bush, so he'll clean my leg."

Fire said, "No."

"Just wait. I'll get Water and she'll drown you."

So she went to Water and said, "Water, drown Fire, so she'll burn the Village, so it'll beat Wolf, so he'll bite Goat, so he'll eat Bush, so he'll clean my leg."

Water said, "No."

"Just wait. I'll get Horse and he'll drink you."

She went to Horse and said, "Horse, drink Water, so she'll drown Fire, so she'll burn the Village, so it'll beat Wolf, so he'll bite Goat, so he'll eat Bush, so he'll clean my leg."

Horse said, "Okay."

So Horse began to drink Water. Water ran and drowned the Fire, Fire leaped and burned the Village, the Village ran and beat the Wolf, the Wolf ran and bit the Goat, the Goat ran and ate the Bush, the Bush shook itself and cleaned Chicken's leg.

And Chicken went on to the bazaar.

—Bosnia (Roosevelt)

Baka and Dika

Long ago there lived two friends named Baka and Dika who each had one single chicken. One day, Dika's chicken wouldn't lay an egg. So she went to borrow an egg from Baka. But Baka said, "What am I, a millionaire? I only have one chicken myself. One chicken, one egg. So go home and get an egg from your own chicken."

When Dika got home, her chicken still hadn't laid an egg.

Dika was so mad, she picked up a stick and started thrashing her chicken. The poor bird shrieked and went running out of Dika's house and off down the street in the direction of the king's castle. When she got to the castle, Dika's chicken stood in front of the gate and squawked like a city councilman.

"Take that bird and put it in the stable under the horses hooves," commanded the king. But the next morning, Dika's chicken was standing on a horse's back and squawking like a drill sergeant.

"Take that bird and put it in the royal beehives," commanded the king. But Dika's chicken took all the bees in the royal beehives and hid them under her wings. The next morning, the king asked his royal beekeepers to bring him the dead chicken. But the beekeepers found the royal beehives empty and Dika's chicken crowing like a presidential candidate.

"Bring the bird to me. Place it in the royal bed and I will personally crush it to death," said the king. But when the king lay down in the bed with Dika's chicken, she opened up her wings and out flew the royal bees.

"Anything she wants!" screamed the king. "I'll give her anything if she'll only stop the bees!"

"What I want," said Dika's chicken, "is a big bag of golden corn to eat so that I can lay my mistress golden eggs."

The king commanded his men to bring a bag of golden corn. Dika's chicken put the royal bees back under her wings. Then she gobbled up the golden corn, brought the bees back to the royal beehive, and strutted back home to Dika.

There she clucked proudly and laid an extra large, grade double-A, golden egg. When Dika saw it, she was so excited that she picked it up and ran across the road to show Baka.

"Oooh," said Baka, "what a pretty egg. Can I have one?"

And Dika drew herself up as grandly as she could and said, "No!"

—Bosnia (Roosevelt)

The Sickness of the Wolf

By a certain lake in the forest there was a place where the animals used to gather to talk and tell each other news. One day, the big news was that Wolf had gotten sick. This was news because Wolf was one of the strongest animals in the forest, and he never got sick. Many of the animals wanted to go and visit, to see for themselves—but they were afraid that, even sick, he might still be dangerous.

So they laid low for a few days. But after they still hadn't seen Wolf for a while, a few of the animals got up the courage to go and pay a social call.

Wolf was staying in a cave during his illness, and as the animals came near they could hear him moaning and groaning. "He sounds awful," said the Deer, who had a big heart. "I'd better go in and make him feel better."

So Deer went into the cave. They all waited a while, but Deer didn't come back out. So one by one the animals went into the cave to pay their respects to Wolf. But none of them came back out.

Fox was hanging back, because he suspected a trick. Fox and Donkey were the last two animals waiting to go in. When they got close to the opening of the cave, Fox saw Wolf lurking in the shadows just inside the door. "Uh—where's Deer?" he asked.

"Come in and I'll tell you," said Wolf.

"You can tell me from here," said Fox.

"I can't tell you, my voice hurts too much. Come closer." But Fox wouldn't come any closer.

So Wolf said to Donkey, "You come closer then. I want to tell you something." Donkey stepped inside the cave, and Wolf jumped on her and killed her.

But Fox ran straight home. He was the only one Wolf didn't trick. So people say: Be like the Fox. Beware the sickness of the Wolf.

—Bosnia (Mather)

The Youngest Son and the Queen of Beauty

Long ago there lived a king who had three sons.

One day the king called his sons and told them, "I'm old, and soon I'll be dead. I need someone to take care of the kingdom when I'm gone. The three of you must travel the world, and the one who can bring me back the most beautiful horse, he will be the new king."

The next day, the king gave his sons food, money, and horses—but the youngest son, who was something of a fool, only got a crust of bread, a little jar of wine, and a donkey to ride. The three of them set off on their way around the world. In a few days they came to a place where the road divided three ways, and they agreed to go their separate ways and to come back together at this spot four years hence.

The eldest son went one way, and on it he met an old man who taught him the trade of shoemaking. He worked for the man for four years, and at the end of it he received his wages in a lump sum, with which he was able to buy a beautiful white horse.

The middle son met an old man who had a ranch. He worked for the man for four years, and at the end of that time he received the best horse on the ranch, a magnificent black horse.

The youngest son had nothing but trouble. As he rode his donkey down the third road, it took fright at some noise and threw him off. Before he could get up, the donkey was gone. Night was coming on, so he decided to sleep under a tree.

During the night a noise woke him. Standing beside him was a cat. The cat looked at him and said, "I haven't eaten for three days. Could you give me something to eat?"

The youngest son thought to himself, "All I have is a crust of bread and a little bottle of wine. And she's just a cat. But she talks nice." So he shared his bread and wine.

While they ate, he told the cat his story. She said, "Come with me." The cat took him to her place. He worked for her for four years, until it was time to go meet his brothers at the crossroads.

The two older brothers had beautiful horses. But all the youngest had was a cat. They asked him, "Where's your horse?" and laughed at him.

When they came to their father's kingdom, he asked them all to tell about their journey, and to show their horses. The oldest and the middle brother showed their horses. The youngest son said that he had only brought this cat. The king was furious and said that for this he should die. On the day appointed for the execution, the king asked his youngest son if he had a last wish. He said, "I want to see my cat one more time." Whereupon there appeared a beautiful woman, riding on the most magnificent horse anyone had seen. She said, "I am the Queen of Beauty. A witch transformed me into a cat, but the love of your son set me free. I would like to give him this horse."

The king was impressed. He gave the kingdom to his youngest son, who married the Queen of Beauty, and together they lived happily and ruled wisely.

—Bosnia (Roosevelt)

The Fairy's Clothes

One night a man was going home through the countryside, and as he passed a certain lake he saw a group of water fairies bathing in the water and dancing on the shore. They were naked, and very beautiful, and their dancing had a grace that was not of this world. As the man crept closer to get a better look, he noticed the fairies' clothes in a heap on the shore. He grabbed one of the dresses and hid it in his bag, and when the fairies came to put their clothes back on and fly away, one was left behind. Without her clothes she had lost her powers, and she had to go with the man back to his house, where she lived as his servant. He gave her ordinary clothes, and in them she seemed like an ordinary human woman, except that she was more beautiful, and she could work harder. But she never smiled, and she never, ever danced.

One day there was a wedding in the village, and everyone was expected to be there. The man went with his beautiful servant. People danced and drank. When the man had drank more than his fill, the fairy came to him and whispered that she would like her own clothes, so that she could dance.

The man remembered how beautiful her dancing was, and he wanted to see her dance again. But he was afraid to give her clothes back because it would give her back her magic powers. So he told the other villagers to close all the doors and windows, and his servant-girl would dance. He went to his house and got her clothes from where he had hidden them. Then they closed all the doors and windows. She put on the clothes, and she began to dance.

Everything at the wedding feast slowed down and stopped altogether. Everyone there was entranced by the fairy's dancing. Soon she began to spin, faster and faster, until suddenly . . . she vanished. The doors and windows could not hold her. She was gone.

But she left behind her curse. For holding her against her will she cursed the village, so that hailstorms came and ruined their crops year after year.

The people went to the church and got stone from the holy altar to place in the hollow of a tree that was sacred to the fairies. That broke the curse.

—Bosnia (Roosevelt)

Nasruddin Hodja

Nasruddin Hodja is a folktale hero whose humorous adventures are known all over the Muslim world. Here are some Nasruddin tales from Bosnia.

Once upon a time, Nasruddin Hodja climbed a tree to cut off a bough. He sat on the bough, faced the trunk, and began to saw. A stranger passing looked up and noticed this operation. He called up to Nasruddin, "Don't sit that way, friend. You'll fall and injure yourself."

Nasruddin said, "What are you, a fortune-teller? Get along and mind your own business."

The stranger went on down the road. In a few minutes, the bough was sawn through and Nasruddin came crashing down with it.

As he lay on the ground the thought came to him: "That man *was* a fortune-teller. If he knew that I was going to fall, then perhaps he knows when I'm going to die."

He got up in a hurry and limped away after the stranger. When he caught up with him he said, "Friend, I see that you are a prophet. Tell me then—when am I going to die?"

The stranger had no idea what Nasruddin was talking about, but just to get rid of him he answered, "You'll die on your way to the mill."

From then on, every time Nasruddin took his corn to the mill he would think about the stranger's words. One day he was on his way to the mill and he felt a pain in his chest. It was gas, but Nasruddin decided that this was his appointed time to die, just as the fortune-teller had predicted. So he lay down in the road, closed his eyes, and waited for the end. The pain went away and he grew quite relaxed.

"If this is death," he thought, "it's really not as terrible as they say."

After a while he heard some snorting and grunting close by his ear. He opened his eyes and saw a group of pigs with their snouts in his bag of corn.

Nasruddin lifted his head and said reproachfully, "When Nasruddin Hodja was alive, pigs didn't eat from people's bags of corn."

—Bosnia (Roosevelt)

The Sound of the Coins

Once there was a rich man who hired a poor man for ten silver coins to cut his wood. The poor man chopped while the rich man watched.

But the rich man fancied that he himself was a great woodcutter. Every time the poor man swung the axe, the rich man grunted and puffed as if he was actually doing the work.

When the job was done, the rich man was tired out from grunting and puffing and pretending to swing the axe. When the poor man asked for his wages, the rich man refused to pay. "I did most of the work," he insisted.

They argued but couldn't agree. Finally they decided to go to Nasruddin Hodja, and to let him be the judge.

They explained the problem to Nasruddin. Nasruddin asked the rich man to give him the coins. Then Nasruddin began to drop the coins one by one on the floor.

"The sound of the coins hitting the floor is your pay for grunting and puffing," he told the rich man.

And then to the poor man: "And for doing the work, the coins go to you."

—Bosnia (Roosevelt)

Timing Is Everything

One day, a young man came to Hodja, wanting to become his student. Hodja saw some potential in the young man and accepted him. The next morning Hodja gave the young man one of his most beautiful jugs and sent him to the next village to bring some water. The way was very long, but at noon he came to the village and filled the jug full. On his way back, with the heavy jug, the student stepped into a hole and stumbled. The jug slipped out of his hands and broke into a thousand pieces. In the afternoon he came back to Hodja with empty hands and told him what happened.

Hodja did not say anything to him that night. The next morning he woke up his student early in the morning. Hodja took the biggest stick he had and started beating his student till the stick broke. The young man cried and cried. Finally Hodja gave his student another jug and sent him to the village. At noon, he arrived there and filled up the jug with water. On his way back, he was extremely careful. In the afternoon, he brought the jug to Hodja, full and undamaged.

Hodja told the student that he had done a good job, and that he had learned his first lesson. The young man asked, "But Master, why did you say nothing to me about the broken jug yesterday when it happened, but you woke me up this morning with a beating?"

"Timing is everything," answered Hodja. "Yesterday you were thinking only of your shame, so a beating would have accomplished nothing. But today you were thinking of the work you had before you, and the beating helped your concentration."

—Bosnia and Herzegovina (Mather)

Tamurlane's Gift

Once the Emperor Tamurlane ordered that a gift be given to the people of the Turkish village called Aksehir. He turned one of his bull elephants over to the people of Aksehir, ordering them to take good care of it. But soon the elephant began to run wild in the town, doing much damage to property, as well as becoming a burden on the people, who were too poor to feed it properly. "This is no gift," said the townspeople. "It's a disaster!"

One day a group of townspeople came to visit Hodja Nasruddin with a request.

"This elephant is not a gift," they cried, "It's a disaster! Please, go to Tamurlane and ask him to take it back."

Then Hodja said, "Let's form a committee. Let's all go together. I'll serve as your spokesman." So a committee was formed, consisting of about fifteen prominent citizens of Aksehir. Hodja joined them, and they set out to visit the emperor.

But these people were terrified of Tamurlane. One by one, they slipped away from the caravan and sneaked off back to Aksehir. Each one had an excellent excuse: "I've forgotten my tobacco-box at home," "I forgot to pay my taxes," "I've got to pass water," and so on and so on. Hodja never even noticed that his committee was melting away. Assuming that they were right behind him, Hodja briskly strode into Tamurlane's tent and began to make his plea.

"Sir," he proclaimed. "This bull elephant is not a gift. It's a—" A little breeze tapped him on his shoulder, and turning his head, he suddenly noticed that none of his committee were there behind him. Since he had already begun his plea, he had to continue, but he made certain adjustments: "It's a very great gift," he choked. "The people of our town are very grateful for the bull elephant. They are happy beyond words, but there only one slight problem, which could, God forbid, result in disastrous consequences, if not addressed. The animal is lonesome and unhappy. We would like your Majesty to consider giving the people of the town a female elephant as a companion for him, so he'll be more contented and less liable to do mischief."

Tamurlane was delighted to hear this flattering plea. "All right," he said graciously. "I shall grant the people's wish, as soon as possible."

Hodja went back to Aksehir. There the townspeople gathered around him, asking anxiously, "Please, tell us, what happened?"

"Rejoice, my friends, I have great news for you," beamed Hodja. "To soften the effects of the male disaster, the emperor has agreed to provide us with a female disaster to keep it company!"

—Bosnia (Mather)

Nasruddin and the Kadija

A long time ago there was a headman of a village in Bosnia, and this man was called the Kadija. Everybody who had problems or had to report something bad that happened in the village had to come to this man.

One day this Kadija invited Nasruddin Hodja, who was also an important man in the village, to join him for dinner. But Nasruddin refused to go. He knew that if he went, the Kadija would make a fool out of him, because the Kadija was a clever man.

So the Kadija had to come up with a better plan. He told his messenger, Chezir, to meet Nasruddin in the marketplace on Thursday morning, because Thursday was the market day in town and Nasruddin could always be found there shopping. He told Chezir to approach Nasruddin and to slap him across the face in front of all the villagers.

On Thursday Chezir went to the bazaar and saw Nasruddin. He walked right up to him and slapped him across the face. Then he ran back to the Kadija's house.

Nasruddin knew who had slapped him, and he went straight away to the Kadija's house to report what happened. "So, Hodja, it's you, come in," said the Kadija. "You've finally come to visit me."

"I just came to report your messenger," said Nasruddin. "He slapped me at the bazaar today, in front of all the people."

Now the Kadija had already talked to his messenger and told him that when Nasruddin came to report what happened, the messenger should tell him that he had some kind of illness. Every month when the moon was full he had to hit somebody.

And so Chezir told Nasruddin what the Kadija had told him to say. But Nasruddin turned to the Kadija and said, "I don't care if he's a werewolf, he's still your servant, and I think you should punish him for what he did."

"You're right," said the Kadija. "It's only right that he should pay you a golden coin. Let him go to his house and get the money for you."

And the Kadija winked at his messenger, as if to say, "Go, and I'll take care of him." So Chezir left, and he didn't come back.

Nasruddin was patient and waited. He waited and waited for an hour, then two, then three hours, but Chezir still wasn't back yet. Nasruddin's patience started wearing away. "Where is that lunatic messenger?" he asked the Kadija. But the Kadija didn't answer. He asked a few more times, and still the Kadija just kept pouring him more tea.

Finally Nasruddin Hodja had had enough. He stood up and slapped the Kadija across the face as hard as he could. "When Chezir comes back, just tell him to give the money to you." And he went home.

The Kadija was angry, but there was nothing he could do about it. Nasruddin had followed the Kadija's own rules, and he got the best of the Kadija that time.

—Bosnia (Mather)

Two Friends (1)

Two friends were taking a walk. On the side of the road they saw a purse. Coming closer, they saw that it was full of money.

One of the friends grabbed it and put it in his pocket, saying, "I have a purse full of money!"

His friend said, "Don't say 'I,' say 'We.' It belongs to us, since we found it together."

"No way," said the first friend. "I saw it first, I picked it up first, it's mine. I'm keeping it."

Just then a stranger ran up to them. "That's my purse," he said. "I saw you put it in your pocket. You're a thief! Police! Help!"

"Oh dear," said the first friend. "What are we going to do?"

"Don't say, 'We,'" said the second friend. "Say, 'I.' You picked it up, it's yours. And everything that goes with it."

Two Friends (2)

Two friends were out walking on a country road. Suddenly a bear came out of the trees and came running at them. The first friend was much faster than the other. He ran straight for a tree and climbed up high; then he sat on a branch and shook with fear.

The second friend didn't have time to run. So he dropped to the ground and lay there with his eyes closed, playing dead.

The bear went up to him and touched his face with its paw. The man never moved. The bear touched the man's nose with its paw, then it leaned over and began to sniff him, up one side and down the other. It sniffed his neck and put its nose right in the man's ear. Finally, getting no response, the bear wandered away.

The man in the road lay still for a long time. When he finally opened his eyes and looked around, he went to the tree and called up, "You can come down now. The bear is gone."

His friend climbed down. "I'm so glad to see you're alive," he said. The second man said nothing. They walked on in silence.

A little while later the first man tried to break the ice. "I saw that bear putting its mouth up to your ear as if it wanted to tell you something," he joked. "What was it saying to you?"

"Not much," said the second friend. "It just said, 'That guy in the tree—he's not much of a friend, is he?'"

—Albania (Roosevelt)

The Dark Place

A long time ago a king and his army were wandering all over the world looking for treasure. They came to a place on the earth where it is always dark, always night. The horses took fright and ran away, so the king and his soldiers had to go on by foot. Up ahead they thought they could make out some kind of castle. But then the darkness grew deeper and they weren't certain. It was so dark that they couldn't see their hands in front of their faces. They found themselves walking over a field of what seemed like sharp stones. Then they heard a voice. It said, "Those who pick up these stones will be sorry. And those who don't pick up any will still be sorry."

The king and his men didn't know what to do. Some of them thought they would reach down and grab just one or two of the stones. The stones were sharp, and in the darkness it seemed as if they were cutting their fingers. Someone shouted that perhaps the stones were poisoned. There were groans, cries, confusion, clashing sounds of soldiers in arms backing into one another. They broke and ran for the borders of the country of day.

When the king and his army were safely back in the light, the few who had saved some of the stones from the dark place brought them out to look at them. They found diamonds, rubies, emeralds, sapphires, and all sorts of precious stones of astonishing size and brilliance.

And the ones who had taken the stones were sorry because they hadn't taken more. And the all the rest were sorry too, because they had taken nothing.

—Serbia (Roosevelt)

The Grandmother's Eyes

Once upon a time there was a shepherd boy who tended his flock on the slopes of a rugged and lonely mountain. One day he fell asleep when he was supposed to be watching, and when he awoke, his sheep were gone, every single one. Without his sheep he was ashamed to go back to his village, so he went deeper and deeper into the mountains, searching for them. He saw no one and nothing for days, until finally, exhausted and starving, he saw the light of a fire in the evening twilight.

When he came closer, he saw an old *babine*—a grandmother. Her eyes were empty sockets— she was blind as a stone. But she had all of his sheep, and many more as well, herded close together in the clearing and bleating as if in terror. He wanted to step forward into the clearing and reclaim his own, but he couldn't move. There was something about the old grandmother that froze him where he stood. Suddenly, as he watched from his hiding place, he heard her mutter some magic words—and when he looked again, all his sheep were lying skinned and roasted on the ground. The smell of burning mutton gathered thickly around him. "I think I'll just stay right here," the boy thought to himself.

The old grandmother took one of the roasted sheep and began to peel off the meat with her bare hands and stuff it in her mouth. She ate that whole sheep and gnawed the bones clean, and then she lay down and began to snore. When the old grandmother was snoring louder than all the night birds and tree frogs and crickets put together, the shepherd boy snuck out into the clearing and stole back one of his own sheep. He took it to his hiding place and ate until he was tired. Then he went to sleep.

The shepherd boy woke up at dawn and finished the rest of that roasted sheep. Then he kept watch on the old blind grandmother as she moved around the clearing, cutting wood for her fire and eating more of his sheep. He stole back another sheep from her during the day when she went a little ways down the hill to fetch water, and he ate that sheep all through that day. He finished it after nightfall, when the old woman's snoring filled the clearing.

The next morning he woke up hungry again. The grandmother seemed as if she was still asleep, and the shepherd boy crept into the clearing to grab another of the roasted sheep. Suddenly, without any warning, the old grandmother was upon him, riding him like a mule with her heels in his side. "Who are you?" she cried. "Are you an angel or a devil?"

"An angel," he said.

"Well then, my angel," said the grandmother. "If you're an angel, there's a special place in the mountains where you can go for me. It's the place where heaven and earth are joined together. Take some of my sheep with you as an offering. When you get there, another angel will come to meet you and want to wrestle with you. If he wins, he will kill you, and if you win, he will offer you anything in heaven or earth. But there is only one thing you can take from the angel: a new set of *babine oci*—grandmother's eyes."

"What if I refuse to wrestle?"

"Then he'll kill you."

"What if I refuse to go?"

"Then I'll kill you."

"Then I'll go."

"Swear you'll take nothing from the angel but a new set of grandmother's eyes."

"I swear."

So the shepherd boy went deeper into the mountains, looking for the place where heaven and earth join together. When he found it, an angel was waiting for him. They wrestled all day long, and at evening the shepherd boy got the angel down on the ground with his wings pinned to his sides.

"What do you want from me—silver, gold, or precious stones?"

The shepherd boy said, "Nothing but a set of *babine oci*—grandmother's eyes."

"Anything but that!" shrieked the angel, but the shepherd boy twisted his wings and the angel gave in. The shepherd boy returned to the old grandmother and gave her the new set of eyes. Suddenly the earth began to shake. The sky grew black and the air filled with smoke and ash. Then, standing before him was no old grandmother, but a beautiful young girl with eyes as clear as water. She looked at the shepherd boy with love and gratitude, and she gave him everything the angel could have given him, as well as things no angel could give.

—Serbia (Roosevelt)

Grandmother March

Sweet Grandmother March was sleeping in her soft bed in her house underground. Outside the sun shone and a warm wind blew, and one bee rose up and flew and it landed on the nose of Grandma March. She sneezed and woke up.

"Uh-oh! Now it's hot, the bees are flying around, and I am still sleeping. Soon they will come to me, my sweet grandchildren April and May, and I haven't done anything for them—I didn't even clean the house!"

Grandmother March got up from her bed and started cleaning the house. She was so happy that her grandchildren were coming. When she got tired and she stopped for a break, she took a deep breath, and the wind from her mouth stirred the dead leaves on the forest floor and stripped off the dead leaves that were left on the trees.

Grandmother March started to feel more comfortable. She started to laugh, and from her laughter the ground got warmer. She started walking from field to field, planting flowers everywhere she went. She walked all day long, until she got tired. Then she stopped to see what she had done today. But when she saw how much was left to be done, she began to cry and pull her hair, and the cold wind and rain lashed the bare tree limbs.

For two days she did nothing but cry. On the third day Grandmother March was still sad, but she remembered about her grandson April, so she jumped up and started cleaning again. She was cleaning very quickly, but even so she started crying again. Grandmother March cried all day long, but suddenly one beautiful bird came by with a letter in its beak. The letter was from her grandson April. April sent her a letter to tell her that he would be coming soon.

Grandmother was reading the letter from her grandson, and she was crying and laughing at the same time. She hadn't even finished the letter when her grandson arrived. Grandma March was so happy to see him. She told her grandson that she was tired of waiting for him, but now he was here and she could take a nap.

Now everywhere the forest was full of life, and the sun was shining every day and flowers sprang out of every patch of earth, and everybody was saying "It's spring, It's spring." From her bed in her underground house, Grandmother March watched with pride as her grandson April went about making everybody happy.

—Bulgaria (Mather)

The Pity

A long time ago in a little village, there lived a father with his two sons. They often went to the forest to chop wood for the fire. But the father was old, and one winter day he fell ill and was too weak to go to the forest. So he said to his sons, "My sons. I can't come with you to the forest today. You must go yourselves and chop wood and bring it home in the cart, lest we freeze to death."

The older son said, "But father, we have never been to the forest by ourselves. What if the cart breaks down, what will we do?"

"Don't worry, my sons. Just call 'the Pity.' It will help you."

Reassured, the two boys took the cart and headed into the forest. They chopped plenty of wood and loaded it in the cart, and then they turned the cart for home. But they hadn't gone far when one of the wheels fell off the cart.

They didn't panic. They remembered their father's advice: "Just call 'the Pity.' It'll help you."

So they began to call: "Pity! Pity! Hey, Pity! Over here, Pity!"

They called for hours. Nothing happened.

Finally the two brothers got tired of calling for the Pity to come and help them. The older one started looking at the wheel, and he thought he saw a way to fix it himself. He tried it, and it worked. Soon they were home, and they rushed into the house to tell their father.

"Father, father, we went to the forest and cut wood, but on the way home a wheel came off the cart, and we called the Pity like you told us to but nothing happened so we had to fix the cart all by ourselves."

The father smiled ruefully, and said, "That's the Pity, my sons. That's the Pity."

—Bulgaria (Roosevelt)

Fat Frumos and Ileana Consinzeana

Once upon a time a long, long time ago, there were two emperors—one white and the other green. The white emperor had three sons—Peter, Paul, and Fat Frumos. The green emperor had one daughter, famous for her beauty, and her name was Ileana Consinzeana.

One day the white emperor called his oldest son and said, "Son, I want you to go to the green emperor and ask for his daughter's hand in marriage. Take the biggest, bravest, swiftest horse in the stable. And hurry—you must come back with her in one week."

The oldest son was happy to go, being a big, brave, impatient young hero. He put on his armor and headed straight to the stable to pick out a horse to ride. There were three horses in the stable, and he picked the biggest, bravest, and swiftest. As he was riding out of the stable, there in the doorway stood a little old lady. She begged him for some bread and some water. But the son just ignored her and left in a hurry.

After traveling for two days and two nights, he met a giant dragon with seven heads, each one bigger and uglier than the last. The prince was just reaching down to grab his sword and start fighting when the ugliest head swooped down, swallowed him like a bug, and then ate his horse for dessert.

A week went by, and the white emperor saw that his oldest son hadn't come back. So he called his middle son. Excited to hear about his heroic task, the middle son didn't want to waste a minute. He ran from the palace to the stable, grabbed the most beautiful of the two remaining horses, saddled him and bridled him, and jumped on top. Right outside the stable door was that little old beggar lady.

"Dear son, will you give me something to eat and to drink?"

"Leave me alone, old lady, can't you see that I am in a hurry?" And he galloped away in a cloud of dust.

Traveling for two days and two nights, the middle son came to the seven-headed dragon—except now it had eight heads, from having eaten another king's son. The middle son tried to ride around the dragon, but the dragon caught him while his horse was standing still and swallowed them both in one bite.

After a week passed the emperor called his youngest son, Fat Frumos. The king was very sad because Fat Frumos was neither brave nor strong like his two older brothers. But he was a good-hearted boy, and he was the emperor's son, so he had to go. After hearing about all he had to do, Fat Frumos left with a smile like no one had seen on his face until that day. Walking toward the stable, he thought, "I know that I can show my dad and the rest of them that I can be a big strong fearless hero like my brothers. Maybe then I can even get married and leave this palace."

Right there at the stable door he met the little old beggar lady. "Dear son," she said, "I'm so hungry—can you give me something to eat and drink?"

Fat Frumos said, "Certainly! I'm in a hurry, but I can still share." He gave the beggar lady some bread and some water and turned to go into the stable to fetch his horse to start his journey.

But before he could go, the old lady said, "Thank you, my dear, for giving me food and water. Now I will give you something in return. Please take this little bag. You will find a magic powder in it. Whenever you have a problem, just take out a pinch of the magic powder, throw it in air, and wish for whatever you need."

Fat Frumos took the leather bag and opened it. Inside was a colorful powder that was shining like the sun in midsummer. Fat Frumos went to the stable to pick his horse. But when he got there, there weren't any more big, strong, beautiful horses left—just one skinny, ugly little pony with sores all over his sides. But Fat Frumos remembered what the old lady had said. He took a pinch of powder from the bag and he threw it in the air and he wished that his horse would be stronger and faster than his brothers' horses, and that it would have wings to boot. He hadn't even finished wishing when everything came true, just as he would have wished it had he finished wishing. There in place of the broken-down pony was the handsomest white mare ever seen in that kingdom, with immense wings sprouting from her shoulders. Fat Frumos leaped on her back and away they flew.

In no time at all they reached the border of the white emperor's realm, where they met the dragon with the seven heads—except now it had nine heads from eating yet another king's son. Fat Frumos spurred his horse to rise high in the air above the dragon's heads. He drew his sword, and as the horse darted from place to place, Fat Frumos leaned over and cut off the dragon's nine heads, one by one. Not five minutes later, the dragon was stretched on the ground with his ugly heads lying all around him.

Fat Frumos flew on, and soon he arrived at the palace of the Green Emperor. When the emperor saw Fat Frumos, he was very glad, because he didn't want his lovely daughter Ileana Cosinzeana moping around the palace anymore. He wanted her to get married and starting making grandchildren for him. But before he gave his daughter's hand, he had to see if Fat Frumos was brave, clever, and heroic enough to be his son-in-law. So he told Fat Frumos, "Go in that room over there, and separate the gold dust from the grain by tomorrow at dawn."

Fat Frumos went into that room, and when he saw what he had to do, he trembled. There was a mountain of gold dust and flour, filling the hall from floor to ceiling, and completely mingled together. But the voice of the little old beggar lady came to his mind, and the voice said, "Use the powder when you need it." He took a pinch of the magic powder and he threw it in the air. In the twinkling of an eye, the grain was in one pile and the gold in another. At dawn when the Emperor came to see what Fat Frumos had done, his face lit up and he said, "Take my daughter with my blessing, and take good care of her."

Fat Frumos took Ileana Cosinzeana on the back of his magic horse, and they flew back to the White Emperor's kingdom faster than the wind, and the all the birds in the world were singing behind them with beautiful songs of happiness. When he arrived at the palace and his father saw his son and his new daughter-in-law he was so proud that he ordered everyone in the kingdom to come to their wedding.

And who would refuse an invitation like that? Not me. Even the birds were there, singing beautiful songs of happiness.

—Romania (Mather)

The Three Fawns

Once upon a time there were three fawns who lived with their mother in the forest. One day the mother deer gathered her three babies around her to tell them about the creatures of the wilderness.

"There are friends in the forest," she told them. "And there are enemies as well. So you must be very careful whom you talk to, and whom you pass information to. Now I am going away to look for food, because everything I've saved for us is all used up. I want you to keep the door locked while I am gone. Don't open it to anyone. When I come back I will knock and sing:

> Oh my little ones open the door.
> I come from afar,
> I bring from afar
> All the goodies that ever there are.

"Now promise me, my children," said the mother deer. "Only when you hear me sing this song will you open the door."

Well, it so happened that hiding by the house was an evil old wolf who heard what the mother deer told her babies. He listened to the verses that she sang, and when she was gone, he came to the door. In his best imitation deer voice he sang:

> "Oh my little ones, open the door.
> I come from afar,
> I bring from afar
> All the goodies that ever there are."

But the oldest fawn said, "That's not our mommy. We won't open the door."

So the wolf went to town and found a blacksmith's shop, and he asked the blacksmith to sharpen his tongue. The blacksmith filed the wolf's tongue till it was pointy sharp, and then the wolf went back to the mother deer's house. There he sang in his sweetest, sharpest voice:

> "Oh my little ones, open the door.
> I come from afar,
> And I bring from afar
> All the goodies that ever there are."

The two youngest fawns said, "That's mommy," and they ran to open the door. The eldest fawn said, "I don't think that's our mommy," but he didn't have time to stop his brothers from opening the door. In through the door leaped the evil old wolf, who grabbed the two younger fawns and ate them up. But the oldest fawn jumped out the door and escaped, and he ran to find his mother.

When the mother deer heard what had happened to her two youngest children she was very angry. She was so angry that she invited the old wolf to supper. But first she made a big hole in the floor and in that hole she made a big fire, and on that fire she put a great big pot of boiling water. Then she covered up the hole with a rug, put the table by the rug, and put the wolf's chair by the rug, too.

When the wolf came into the house he said, "Oh what a pretty table you've set, Mrs. Deer. What are we having for dinner?"

"Sit right down and you will see," said the mother deer. She pulled back the chair and the wolf stepped on the rug, and when he did he went straight down into the hole and into the pot of boiling water.

"We are having you for dinner, Mr. Wolf," said the mother deer.

"My dear old friend, don't let me die," cried the wolf.

But the mother deer threw the rug back over the hole to keep the flavor in, and when she opened it up again, she and her only remaining fawn had a great big pot of wolf stew. And that was that.

—Romania (Roosevelt)

Rooster and Fox

One beautiful morning a young rooster jumped on the fence and started to sing his song. Out of the woods came a hungry fox, and he approached the rooster very quietly. When she was right behind the rooster she spoke up. "Good morning," said the fox. "I was just admiring your singing. You have a beautiful voice. But there's just one thing bothering me. I don't know whether you can sing as your father did."

The rooster asked, "So how did my father sing?"

"Oh," said the fox, "He would stand on one leg on the fence, close one eye, and then he'd sing like an angel."

"I can do that too," said the rooster. He closed one eye, stood on one leg, and started to sing.

"That's very good," said the fox. "But your father could really sing. I remember how he used to stand on one leg, close both eyes, and sing like an archangel."

"I can do that too," said the rooster. He closed the other eye and started to sing. At that moment the fox grabbed the rooster, and carried him off into the woods.

When she came to her house the fox was all ready to eat the poor rooster, when the bird spoke up and said, "Clearly you don't have the refinement that your mother had. I remember that she would never have a meal without singing grace."

The fox said, "I am exactly as my mother was." So she closed her eyes, and started to sing grace. At this very moment the rooster hopped out of her mouth and flew away back home. And that's the story of how the rooster and the fox traded tricks.

—Ukraine (Mather)

The Golden Ring

Once there were three brothers. Two of them were smart and the third one was kind of slow. His name was Ivan. One sad day their father died. As he had some money and land, the three brothers had to divide the inheritance among themselves. The first two brothers were cheapskate types, so they took all the money and all that beautiful land. As for Ivan, they gave him nothing but an old, toothless, sway-backed nag.

Every day Ivan's two brothers made him to go work in the fields. The poor boy didn't have anything else to do. The only friend that he had was that ugly horse, and Ivan was always kind and good to him. One day the horse told Ivan. "Don't worry, all the work will be done in time. The only thing that you have to do is pull my tail three times and whisper a magic word in my ear." So Ivan did as he was told. And in a flash, that sway-backed nag turned into a splendid trotter, and Ivan turned into a handsome knight.

At that time there was a king who was trying to find a husband for his daughter. But she disapproved of all the young men who came to their palace. So the king got tired of that and decided to make a challenge for all who would marry his daughter. The first man who could meet the challenge would be the one to marry the princess. The challenge was very difficult. The king put his daughter at the very top of the highest tower in the palace, and there she held a golden ring. The challenge was to get that ring from her hand. Many young men tried, but none of them could do it.

Ivan heard about this competition and decided to try for himself. He told his brothers about his idea, but they just laughed. They couldn't believe that Ivan would try to jump so high on his old broken-down horse. But Ivan didn't listen to them. He took his horse, went out in the field, pulled his horse's tail three times, said the magic word, and turned into handsome knight. He leaped on his horse, now a splendid trotter, and rode to the tower, where the princess was waiting with the golden ring.

Ivan and his magic horse gathered speed and jumped, and just as if the horse had wings, they soared to the very top of the tower, and Ivan snatched the ring from the princess's hand. After that he rode back home, stabled his horse, turned back to his usual scruffy self, and went to bed.

However, while he was sleeping his brothers saw that he had the golden ring. They just couldn't believe that Ivan could have gotten the ring by jumping that high. They assumed that their brother had killed someone and stolen the ring. So they ran straight to the king and told him the whole situation, hoping for a reward for their trouble. The king ordered his soldiers to go arrest Ivan and bring him to the court.

When the king saw Ivan, he couldn't believe that this ragged young man was the one who got the ring. So the king ordered the soldiers to cut off Ivan's head. As the poor boy was going to the place where he was supposed to be executed, his horse came galloping up, already in his magical shape. Ivan jumped on his back, turned into a handsome knight, and they jumped to the top of the tower. The princess stepped out onto the horse's back, and the three of them, man, woman, and horse, floated back to earth as lightly as a feather.

At that moment the king saw that Ivan was really the one who had captured the golden ring. So Ivan married young princess, and they and the magical horse lived happily ever after.

—Ukraine (Mather)

One Eye, Two Eyes, and Three Eyes

Once there was a little girl whose name was Maria. She lived happily with her mother and father. However, one sad day her mom died, and her dad married a very mean lady. Maria's stepmom hated her and made the poor girl do all the hard work around the house. The "new" mother had her own daughters, but she never made them do a thing. One of her daughters had one eye, another one had two eyes, and the third one had three eyes.

Everyday Maria had to go out to the fields and get all the work done, otherwise her stepmom would kick her out of the house. Maria had no friends at all, except for a cow, who was a present from her mother. So Maria took the cow to the field with her every day.

One day as Maria was complaining to the cow about her difficult life, the cow suddenly spoke up and said to Maria, "Don't worry. I can get your work done for you. The only thing you have to do is to climb into my right ear and climb out of my left ear. By the time you get out, all the work will be done."

Maria was surprised, but she did as she was told. She looked in her cow's right ear. It seemed to open up like a door and she walked right in. She walked and she walked through a pleasant dream, and when she walked out another door, it turned out to be her cow's left ear, and all the work was done, exactly as the cow had promised.

And that's the way it went for a long time. But after a while her stepmom started to wonder how could Maria do all the work in time. Every day she would give the poor girl more and more work to do, and Maria always came home early with the work all done. So one day she sent One Eye to spy on Maria.

But Maria was clever. She sang a lullaby, and as she sang, her stepsister's one eye slowly fell shut and she slept. When One Eye woke up, all the work was done. She had to tell her mom that she had failed. The next day the mean stepmom sent her second daughter, Two Eyes. The same thing happened to her. Maria sang a lullaby, and the first eye fell asleep. Then she sang another song, and the second eye fell asleep also. So Maria got all the work done again, and when Two Eyes woke up, Maria and her cow were gone.

When Two Eyes told her mom that she had failed, the woman was furious. She decided to send her Three Eyes to spy on Maria. So the next day the oldest sister went out on the field with Maria. As usual, the girl sang a lullaby, and one eye fell asleep. She sang another song, and the second eye fell asleep too. But she forgot to sing a song for the third eye. And her oldest stepsister was able to see how Maria got all the work done on time.

When Maria came back home she heard her stepmother begging her father to kill the cow. She said that she was dying from some kind of disease, and the only thing that could save her was cow's heart.

At first her dad said, "That's a shame. That cow is Maria's only friend." But the stepmother kept nagging him and badgering him till he gave his permission to kill the cow and take its heart.

When Maria heard his decision she wept and wept. The poor girl didn't know what to do. So she decided to ask her cow. Strange to say, the cow wasn't upset or scared at all. She just said, "After I'm dead, eat none of my meat. No matter how hungry you are, don't taste a bite. But after the rest have picked my bones clean, gather them up and bury my bones in the garden by the house."

So Maria did what she was told, and the very next morning, at the place where the bones of her friend were buried, there grew a beautiful apple tree.

Later that same day, it happened that a very handsome prince was passing by the house where Maria lived. He saw the beautiful apple tree growing in the garden. As he was tired from the long trip, he decided to stop and ask for one of those beautiful apples.

Maria's stepmother welcomed him, and she sent One Eye to go and fetch an apple for the prince. But when the girl reached for the apple, all the branches of the tree rose straight up in the air, so she wasn't able to touch even a single apple.

Then Maria's stepmother sent her second daughter, Two Eyes, and the same thing happened to her. As she reached for an apple, all the branches rose straight up. Maria's stepmother was getting angry. She sent her third daughter, Three Eyes, to fetch an apple for the prince. But again the branches rose straight up in the air, and the third daughter couldn't touch a single apple.

The stepmother was enraged and said she would have the tree cut down. But the prince asked Maria, who was standing quietly off to one side, if she would please go and pick an apple for him. Now when Maria approached the tree, all the branches bowed down and covered her from all sides, so that for a moment no one could see her. And then, after a while, the branches rose up again, and Maria appeared. She had become the most beautiful girl in the world, and she was wearing a dress that shone like the Sun, Moon, and stars.

The prince fell in love with Maria on the spot. He took her back to his palace on horseback—eating apples all the way—and the next day they got married, and they lived happily ever after.

—Ukraine (Mather)

No Accident

The Lubavitch Hasidim* say that some things may look like accident or misfortune, but you never know why or to what purpose they may actually be occurring.

One Shabbos eve, an old man came to the door of a poor Jewish family and said, "I'm hungry, I need something to eat."

All the family had for supper was a pot of soup, and not much of that. But the commandment was that it was forbidden to turn away a stranger on Shabbos. So they invited him in and gave him a bowl of soup.

The old man's hands were shaking. They shook so badly that when he tried to put the spoon in the bowl—"*Trach!*"—he spilled the bowl and the soup went everywhere.

Well, the father knew that if he gave the old man another bowl of soup, then he himself would have to go hungry. But the commandment was the commandment. So he poured the old man another bowl of soup. And as the old man reached out his spoon to the bowl—"*Trach!*"—he spilled it again.

Now the father knew that if he filled the old man's bowl again, then his children would have to go hungry. But the commandment was the commandment. So he filled the old man's bowl again, and sure enough—"*Trach!*"—he spilled it again.

*A religious movement within Eastern European Jewry. Many Hasidim are now U.S. residents.

Meanwhile, just at that moment, at the palace of the czar of all Russias, the czar himself was getting ready to sign a decree against the Jews, legalizing certain persecutions and condemning them to an evil fate. But as the minister brought the proclamation and a bottle of ink to the czar for his signature, the czar's hands suddenly began to shake violently. And when he reached out his pen to dip it in the inkwell—"*Trach!*"—he spilled the ink all over the proclamation.

So the ministers had to prepare a whole new copy of the proclamation to sign. But when they brought it to the czar, and he reached out his pen to dip it in the inkwell, again his hands began to shake violently. And before he could stop himself—"*Trach!*"—down went the inkwell all over that proclamation.

The prime minister turned bright red and began apologizing profusely to the czar, even though it was not he who had ruined the two proclamations. He promised that he would have the document redone right away. The scribes were called, the proclamation was redrafted. But when the prime minister took it from the scribes and turned to present it to the czar, he tripped over his coat and spilled the ink all over the proclamation.

And then all the ministers began to tremble, because they realized that something supernatural was afoot, and the hand of God had reached into their chamber. So they cancelled the decree, and the Jews were spared that day—on account of a simple Jewish family that kept the commandment of charity on the Shabbos.

—Jewish, from the Lubavitch Hasidim (Senn)

Diamonds and Onions

Once there was a wealthy merchant who sailed the seas in search of trade. On one of his voyages his ship was wrecked and he himself was washed up on a distant shore, with only the waterlogged clothes on his back.

As he dragged himself up the beach he began finding stones of unusual brilliance scattered about. Looking more closely, he realized that they were diamonds, and he began filling his tattered pockets with the stones, hoping to sell them in exchange for safe passage home and even a new store of money and goods.

But when he reached the city and showed his discoveries around, the people there said, "Those things? Those are useless to us. We find them everywhere. We line our rock gardens with them."

"But this is astounding! Where I come from these are called diamonds, and they're worth fortunes!"

"Well we don't know where you come from, stranger, but here they're called rocks. Why, to hear you talk, you'd think you'd found onions."

"Onions?"

"Yes, onions."

"What about onions?"

"Well, they're extremely rare and valuable. Most people have only heard tell of them. Why?"

"Oh never mind," said the merchant. So he threw away his diamonds and went and offered himself as an assistant to a wealthy onion merchant. In no time at all he mastered the trade and became an onion dealer himself, amassing what for those parts was a tremendous fortune—many millions of onions.

He never forgot his family and friends back in his former country. But he did forget certain things about their customs. So when he finally got around to outfitting a ship to go home, he took his whole fortune in onions along with him, intending to sell it and give it away to institutions of higher education. And he left the diamonds, which he, too, had come to disdain, lying scattered on the beach.

His family and friends that were still living were overjoyed to see him, but they soon became concerned about his mental health. He kept trying to give them bags of onions and acted as if they should be falling on their knees with gratitude. Instead they just took his gifts straight to the kitchen, where they turned them into soups and stews. He was furious! Who did they think they were, eating up his hard-earned fortune?

Soon he sailed right back to the kingdom of the onion merchants, where his generosity would be better appreciated.

And the Lubavitcher Hasidim say that so it is with us—What we hold to be valuable and what is valuable in G-d's kingdom are two completely different standards. And what the standard will be when we get back home to that heavenly country, we should not be too quick to judge.

—Jewish, from the Lubavitch Hasidim (Senn)

THE MIDDLE EAST

The Inheritance

Once there was a boy named Samer. He lived with his rich father in a beautiful castle.

Samer had a lot of friends his own age, but they didn't really care about Samer. They were only using him for his money. He would give them money to buy sweets or clothing or whatever caught their eye. So they hung around.

Samer's father was well aware that his son's friends were using him. He tried to tell his son, but Samer wouldn't listen.

One day the father took Samer aside and said, "Before long I will be dead. When I'm gone, if you spend all my money and fall into poverty, go to my room. Put a rope around your neck, secure it to the roof beam, and hang yourself."

Before long, Samer's father did pass away. Samer went on spending money on his friends as before, but without his father to manage the estate there soon was nothing left—no money for food or clothing or for anything at all. Samer went to his friends to borrow money, but they shut their doors in his face.

So Samer remembered his father's words. For his honor and that of his family, he would have to kill himself.

He went to his father's room. He stood on a chair, put the rope around his neck, and secured it around the roof beam. Then he kicked away the chair.

Down came the roof beam and a panel of the ceiling along with it, and after the panel came bags of gold and silver and paper money. It almost killed Samer, but not quite—and it knocked some sense into him. He realized that his father hadn't really meant for him to kill himself, but to save him from the fool he had been.

When Samer's friends heard that he had money again, they rushed to his bedside to visit him. "What do you want now?" he asked them.

"We want to be like before—to go out and have fun."

Samer had the servants show his old friends the door.

After that Samer lived prudently, and began to have friends that were true.

—Palestine (Roosevelt)

Ajlooka

Once upon a time there was a mother who lived by herself with her only daughter, Ajlooka. One day Ajlooka asked her mother if she could go to her aunt's house to play with her cousins. Ajlooka's mother said no.

Ajlooka begged to be allowed to go, but her mother said, "No, your aunt doesn't like you."

"No," said Ajlooka, "it isn't so." And she ran out of her mother's house and went straight to her aunt's.

She played with her cousins until evening and then it grew dark. Ajlooka was afraid to go home by herself in the dark. So she asked her aunt if she could stay over the night.

Her aunt said, "No. We've got no space for you."

Ajlooka said, "I'll sleep at the foot of your children's bed."

"No," said her aunt, "you'll keep them awake."

Ajlooka said, "Then I'll sleep on the roof."

"No," said her aunt, "the clothes are up there drying on the line, and you'll knock them down."

Ajlooka said, "Then I'll sleep in the stable with the sheep."

Her aunt said, "No, they'll make noise all night and keep us all awake."

Ajlooka said, "Then I'll sleep in the flowering almond tree."

"No! No! No!" said her aunt. You'll tear off all the blossoms. Ajlooka, nobody invited you here. You're going to have to go home to your mother."

Ajlooka started for home in the dark, but every noise filled her with terror. As she passed the flowering almond tree, she thought she heard footsteps. Her heart leaped into her throat and she grabbed the lowest branch of the tree and pulled herself up.

It was peaceful in the tree, surrounded by the smell of the blossoms, and she began to fall asleep. Suddenly, at the foot of the tree, stood a *wahash*—a desert-dwelling ghoul.

"Get down from that tree," said the *wahash*.

"No," said Ajlooka. "You'll eat me."

"I said, get down!"

But Ajlooka wouldn't get down. So the monster grabbed the branch of the tree that Ajlooka was sitting on and ate it. Ajlooka jumped up to the next branch.

"I said, get down!"

But she wouldn't get down. So the *wahash* ate the next branch. Ajlooka climbed higher, but the *wahash* ate the next branch, and the next. Finally there was only one branch left, at the very top of the tree where the *wahash* couldn't reach her. Ajlooka hung on for dear life.

"Get down!"

But Ajlooka wouldn't get down. "You'll eat me," she said.

"Listen," said the *wahash*. "If you can jump down and get on my shoulders, I'll take you to your mother's house."

"Oh yeah," said Ajlooka, "and what if I fall?"

"Then I'll eat you."

Ajlooka thought about it. Her arms were getting tired. The branch was starting to bend and crack. She said, "Okay."

And she jumped and landed on the shoulders of the *wahash*. He took her to her mother's house. They knocked on the door.

Ajlooka's mother got out of bed. "Who's there?" she cried.

Ajlooka said, "It's me, your daughter, Ajlooka."

"My daughter is at her aunt's house."

"Mother, it's me, I swear it."

"How did you get home?"

"I came by myself."

But her mother didn't believe her. "Something is terribly, terribly wrong," said Ajlooka's mother, and she wouldn't open the door.

So the *wahash* took Ajlooka to his cave and ate her up.

—Palestine (Roosevelt)

Ajlooka and the Gas Seller

There was a very beautiful girl whose name was Ajlooka. She lived on a small farm with her husband and one cow.

One day a gas seller came through the neighborhood calling, "Gas for sale! Gas! Gas for sale!"

Ajlooka needed some gas, so she ran out to meet him. All the neighbors were out in the road buying their gas, but when it came Ajlooka's turn, the gas seller said, "Wait a minute here. You are a very beautiful woman. Tell me, what is your name?"

She told him, "My name is Ajlooka."

The gas seller burst out laughing. "Such a beautiful woman and such an ugly name!"

He saw that Ajlooka was ashamed. So he said, "Listen, my dear, I'm going to give you a beautiful new name, just as beautiful as you are. And you will give me money—or whatever you have."

"I have no money," Ajlooka said, "or not enough for anything so valuable as a new name."

"What do you have then?"

"I have one cow."

"I'll take it."

"But the cow gives us milk and cheese, and that's all my husband and I have."

He said, "But a beautiful name is worth more than silver and gold."

So she gave him the cow. "Wise choice," he said. "Your new name will be Zohor-El-Dar" (which means Hothouse Flower).

"Zohor-El-Dar," she breathed, barely believing her good fortune.

"Now that your name is Zohor-El-Dar," said the gas seller, "you must not open the door for anybody who calls you Ajlooka—not even your husband. Do you understand?"

Ajlooka nodded.

"May Allah the Compassionate, the Merciful, protect you," said the gas seller, and he went away with her cow.

That night when Ajlooka's husband came home, the door was locked. He knocked hard. "Ajlooka, it's me. Open the door!"

But she made no sound, and she wouldn't come to the door. Their neighbors came out, laughing and giggling, and told him about the gas seller and the cow. "She got no gas, but he sold her a new name. She won't answer to anything but Zohor-El-Dar."

"Zohor-El-Dar?"

Ajlooka opened the door with a radiant smile. "Yes, dear?"

"You sold our only cow for a name? Can we eat names? Are you going to go to the barn in the winter and bring me a meal of Zohor-El-Dar?"

Ajlooka cried, "But I had an ugly name!"

Her husband said, "I'm leaving! You can take your beautiful name and eat it three times a day, but I'm not coming back till I meet three women as stupid as you, and that will take forever!"

He turned on his heel and stormed off. He soon came to a group of women standing in the road. They called him by name and asked where he was going in such a terrible hurry.

Still furious, he burst out, "To hell!"

"To hell?" the first woman cried. "Wait just a moment. I have a package for you to deliver to my husband. I'm sure you'll find him there."

"Oh, wait for me too," cried the second woman. "My older sister was a terrible gossip. I have some news to write down for her."

The third woman said, "I have some food and some money for you to bring to my eldest son, who was killed in a tavern brawl. Just wait right there."

And all three women ran off to their houses to make up their little gift packages for their relatives in hell. Ajlooka's husband took the packages and went straight home to his wife.

They made several good meals of the food, and with the money they bought a new cow. And they had a little left over to buy some gas.

—Palestine (Roosevelt)

The Grandfather's Plate

A long time ago there was a well-to-do family living in a neat, well-kept house in a small village in Palestine. In addition to the husband and his wife, there was one son and the husband's father, who was getting on in years.

The husband's father was so old, in fact, that his fingers had begun to shake. When the family sat at the table to eat, the grandfather would spill soup on the table. This would make his daughter-in-law very angry. Sometimes, too, his shaking fingers would knock the plate onto the floor. Then she would scream and curse at him, and he would hang his head in shame. The husband would try and come to his father's defense, but she would only shout him down.

Finally she made the old grandfather sit by the fire, away from the table. But this only made things worse. For without the table to support his plate, he would spill whole servings of soup on himself and then drop the plates to the hearth, where they would break into little pieces.

After losing a couple of plates in this way, the wife said coldly, "I will not stand for you to break all my good dishes. I'm going to have a plate made out of wood so you can spill food on yourself and drop it to your heart's content." And she went to the bazaar and got a wooden plate made for her father-in-law. She made him eat from the wooden plate in front of the fire—and his shame grew deeper.

One day, their little son Ahmed was playing in the garden. He found a piece of an old stump and began carving it with his pocket knife. After a while his mother came out and saw him. "Ahmed," she asked, "what do you think you're doing?"

"I'm making a plate out of wood," he said, "so that when you and my father are old I can put soup in the plate and make you sit by the fire."

Her son's words filled the mother with shame. From then on the old grandfather sat at the table with the family and ate off the same plates as they did.

—Palestine (Roosevelt)

The Three Cows

A long time ago there were three cows, one black, one red, and one white; they were best of friends and always grazed together. And close by their pasture there was a lion. Though the lion was very strong, he wasn't strong enough to kill all three cows at once, or even two at once. The friends protected each other and wouldn't let the lion come near.

One day the lion came to where the three cows were grazing, and he got the black and white cows off to the side of the pasture and said, "Listen. I'm really your friend. I only want to help you. And I want you to know that that red cow over there is nothing but trouble. Her bright red color stands out at a distance. With her around, your enemies will always know where to find you. Better let me kill her and eat her so you two will be safe."

The black and white cows thought about it for a while. Suddenly the red cow didn't look like a friend anymore—she looked like danger. They told the lion, "Go ahead and kill her, Mr. Lion, so we two will be safe." So the lion killed the red cow and ate her.

Time passed, and when the lion was hungry again, he came to the white cow and told her, "Listen. I hate to tell you this, but that black cow is trouble. Your enemies can see her at any distance." The white cow thought about it, and then she told the lion to go ahead and kill the black cow so that she would be safe. The lion was happy to oblige.

Not long after that, the lion came to where the white cow was grazing by herself. "Oh dear," said the lion, "there's nobody left in this field but you. And you know, by yourself you stand out at any distance. I'm going to have to kill you and eat you too."

The white cow looked at the lion in despair. "I was already eaten," she said, "the day you ate the red cow."

—Egypt (Roosevelt)

In parts of the Middle East, Nasruddin Hodja is known to people as Gioha. Here are a few Gioha stories from Yemen and Syria.

Gioha Teaches the People to Pray

Once upon a time there was a country where the people had forgotten how to pray. They knew that they were lacking in this area, so they were eagerly waiting for someone to come and teach them the proper way.

One day Gioha came to visit this country. The people asked him to teach them how to pray. Gioha agreed that he would show them. "You must do and say everything exactly as I do," he told them. They nodded.

Gioha got down on his hands and knees and began to do the Muslim prayers. He put his face down to the wooden floor with such pious devotion that his nose got wedged in a crack of the floorboards. *"Bismallah, al-Rahman, al-Raheem,"* he chanted. Then suddenly he screamed, *"My nose!"*

All the people behind him screamed out along with him, *"My nose!"*

Gioha screamed again, *"My nose!!"* And the people all screamed louder, *"My nose!!"*

When he finally got his nose loose from the crack in the floor, he was too embarrassed to tell the people what had happened. So to this day the people of that country pray exactly as Gioha taught them: *"Bismallah, al-rahman, al-raheem—My nose!!"*

—Yemen (Roosevelt)

The Most Intelligent Donkey

One time the king received a donkey as a gift from a friend. All of the friends of this friend of the king were praising the donkey and saying extravagant things so that the king would think well of the gift and of the giver.

When it was Gioha's turn to speak, he said, "This is the most intelligent of donkeys. Indeed, this donkey is so intelligent that in three months time, I could teach it to read."

Everyone present fell silent, afraid that Gioha had overstepped himself. The king said, "Gioha, if you can teach this donkey to read, I'll give you his weight in gold. And if you can't, then I'll make you wish you'd never been born." All eyes turned to Gioha.

He said, "Your majesty, I agree to the challenge, but not for the gold, nor for my own pride, but for the honor of this noble beast, and of the man who gave him to you."

Well, after three months, Gioha came to the court of the king to demonstrate the accomplishments of the marvelous donkey. The king and his council all sat in a circle with the donkey at the head. Gioha brought a great big leather-bound book, opened it, and set it on the ground in front of the donkey. The donkey looked at the page for a moment, then he reached down and turned the page with his teeth. Then he looked up at Gioha and made a soft snorting sound, like a critic.

The donkey looked at the next page, reached out and turned it, and again made this soft snorting sound, full of discernment and sensibility. The king and his court burst into applause, and they ordered that Gioha should be immediately given the donkey's weight in gold.

Afterwards, back in their village, Gioha's friends asked him to please tell them what methods he had used to accomplish this astonishing feat of donkey pedagogy.

Gioha replied, "It was quite simple. I got a deerskin, tanned it and stretched it and cut it into pages, and bound it into a book. Then behind every page I put oats. I placed this book before the donkey. Soon he realized that when he turned the page he would find food. And when he didn't find food, then he would look at me and snort. And that's what he just did. He wasn't criticizing the book, my friends. He was criticizing his dinner."

So to all our school age friends, I say: Don't be like Gioha's donkey—don't just read for the oats!

—Syria (Mather)

The Answer to Everything

Once a traveling wise man came to Gioha's village and issued a challenge. Anyone who can answer all the questions I ask him with a single answer, that one I will call Master." The people directed him to Gioha. So he went to Gioha's house and told him, "I have forty questions to ask you. If you can answer all forty questions with a single answer that applies equally to all, then I will call you Master."

So the stranger asked Gioha the forty questions. And Gioha said, "You want a single answer to all those questions?"

"That's right."

"Well then. The one true answer to all those questions is . . . I don't know."

And the wise man called Gioha Master.

Gratitude

Gioha lost his donkey. All the while as he was looking for it, he kept loudly thanking God. "Thank God, thank God, thank God," he kept repeating with each and every step. His friends who witnessed this became curious.

"What are you doing, Gioha?" they asked.

"I'm looking for my donkey," Gioha replied.

"Is he lost?"

"Yes, he is, thank God."

"So if your donkey is lost, why are you thanking God?"

"Because if I had been riding him when he got lost, I'd be lost too!"

—Syria (Mather)

Hassan and the Swan Woman of the Island of the Djinn

Once upon a time in a little village in Yemen there lived a wealthy man named Haroun who had a simple-hearted young friend named Hassan. Haroun knew the way to an island of the *djinn*—the fire spirits—where there was a mountain all of gold at the top. But Haroun was too old and fat to get to the gold. So he called on his young friend Hassan. He offered to split the gold if Hassan would come with him to the island and go up the mountain to get it. Hassan said that he would try.

So Haroun and Hassan went to the island of the *djinn*. At the foot of the mountain, Haroun brought out a long leather bag. "Get inside," he told Hassan, "and the eagles will carry you to the top of the mountain. Fill the bag with gold and throw it down to me. Then I'll throw the bag back up and let the eagles carry you down again, and we'll go home and enjoy our riches."

Hassan did as Haroun instructed. The eagles came down at a certain time and carried the bag up to the top of the mountain. Then Hassan got out of the bag, filled it full of gold, and threw it back down the mountain to Haroun. But when Haroun looked in the bag and saw the gold, his heart darkened. "By rights all this should be mine," he thought. "Why should I share it with that ignorant oaf?"

"I'll just take this home and come back later," he called to Hassan. And Haroun jumped in his boat and hurried back to the mainland.

When he realized that Haroun would not come back, Hassan began to explore the top of the mountain. He walked over fields of gold and precious stones until he came to a house. He went inside the house, and there he found seven girls. They greeted him kindly, gave him food, and told him that he could stay with them from there on and be like their brother.

The next morning the girls got up and got ready to go to work. Before they went they told Hassan, "Stay and enjoy yourself—anything in this house is yours, except for one thing: Don't open the door to our room."

Hassan agreed, but of course they had not been gone ten minutes when he opened the door to their room and stepped inside.

He found himself by a beautiful crystal lake surrounded by forests and mountains. Seven swans came flying over the treetops and glided down onto the surface of the lake. They came to shore and stepped out of their coats of feathers and became the most beautiful women that Hassan had ever seen. They bathed in the lake for a while, then they got back into their feather coats and flew away over the treetops.

Hassan fell hopelessly in love with the oldest and most beautiful of the swan women. Every day when his adopted sisters went to work he would open the door to their room and watch them bathe in the lake. One day one of his sisters noticed that Hassan was losing weight. She asked him what was wrong. He confessed to her that he had opened the door to their room and fallen in love with one of the swan women. "But," he said hopelessly, "they're not people—they're *djinn*."

"I told you not to open the door," she said.

"But I did," he said. "And now I need your help."

"Alright," she said, "here is an idea for you. Go into the room at the usual time, and when you see the swans take off their feather coats and dive back in the lake, go down to the shore and steal the coat of the one you love best. Then when the others fly away you may take her with you."

The next day Hassan did as his sister suggested. He watched as the swans flew over the tree-tops and landed on the lake; he watched them swim to shore and take off their swan coats; and when they dove back into the lake to bathe he slipped down to the shore and stole the feathers of the one he loved. When they were finished bathing they climbed out and put on their feathers, except for his beloved, who went up and down the shore looking frantically for hers. The others couldn't wait and flew away without her. Then Hassan stepped out and asked her to marry him, and she had to agree.

He put her feather coat in a suitcase and locked it, and then Hassan and his swan wife were married and went to live by themselves. After a year and a day she gave birth to a baby boy. Hassan wanted to take his wife and baby and go to visit his mother. But on the way he got an urgent message from his adopted sisters on the island of the djinn, wanting him to come and visit them.

So Hassan went home and gave the locked suitcase to his mother, saying, "Whatever you do, don't give the key to this suitcase to my wife." He put his wife and baby in the care of his mother and he set off for the island to visit his sisters.

While he was gone, there was a wedding in the village for the son of the sheikh. Hassan's wife went to the wedding, and at the party afterwards she began to dance. Everyone in the village was astonished at how she danced. She told the people, "Listen   Hassan's mother has a certain suitcase, and in that suitcase is a certain dress, and if I had that dress I could really show you how to dance."

Hassan's mother protested, but the sheikh ordered her to go and bring the suitcase and the key. Hassan's wife took the suitcase and grabbed her baby and went to the women's bath. The people were waiting to see her dance, but all that came out the door of the women's bath was a great white swan, with a baby hanging from its beak, who flew off over the ocean toward the island of the djinn.

Her father, the king of the djinn, was angry with her because she had allowed herself to be taken by a mortal. So he locked her in a room alone with her baby.

When Hassan came home to his village, his mother told him what had happened at the wedding. Hassan turned around and started straight back for the island. On his way he met two brothers who were having an argument. He stopped and asked what was the matter. "Our father died," they said, "and he left us this hat and this sword. And both of us want both things, and we can't figure out how to divide them."

Hassan asked, "What's so special about this hat and this sword?"

They told him that if you wore the hat, no one could see you though you could see them; and that if you hit the ground with the sword you could go anywhere at the speed of thought, even to the island of the djinn. Hassan told them, "I'll throw a stone, and the first one who brings it back will have both the hat and the sword."

They agreed. So Hassan threw a stone as far as he could. They threw down the hat and sword and ran to fetch it, and when they did, Hassan grabbed the hat and put it on, and he grabbed the sword and hit the ground with it and in a flash he was there on the island of the djinn. No one could see him, but he could see everyone, so he went door to door knocking until he heard his wife's voice answer—then he hit the ground with his sword and thought of her and found himself in a flash inside the locked door. The baby started crying, "Baba, baba," and she said, "Who is it? Where is Hassan?" He took off the hat and stood before her. They embraced and she said she was sorry for leaving, but he just took her in his arms and held the baby and tapped the sword on the ground, and at the speed of thought they were home again, and they lived happily ever after.

—Yemen (Roosevelt)

Does Your Father Have Horns on His Head?

Once upon a time there was a foolish boy who lived all alone with his old mother. One day his mother told him to butcher their cow, take all the parts to town to sell, and to bring her back all the money. He butchered the cow, and took the parts to town in a wagon. Many people offered to buy the beef, but each one said, "I have no money today. Give me the meat and I'll pay you tomorrow."

At last he had given away all the meat. He had no money, and all he had left in the wagon was the cow's skin and its head. No one was interested in either one, so the foolish boy started for home.

On the way, a dog began barking at him. He said, "You want the head? Okay, here. But I want the money tomorrow." He threw the cow's head to the dog, and it stopped barking.

A little further on he saw a lizard shaking its head at him. "You want the skin? Okay, here. But I want the money tomorrow." He threw the cowskin to the lizard and went on home.

"Where's the money?" asked his poor old mother.

"They all said they'd pay me the money tomorrow," he said.

"My poor foolish darling," said his mother. "We'll be lucky if we see one copper penny of that money."

The next day he went back to town to collect the money, but wherever he looked for them, his customers were not to be found. Finally on the way home he saw the dog. He chased it, but it ran away. Then he came to the rock where the lizard sat. He chased it, but it slipped away between the rocks. The boy put his hand in after it, and he heard something jingle. He reached down further and pulled out a jar full of gold.

"At least somebody's willing to pay me," he said, and he took a couple of coins from the jar, just to cover the price of the cowskin. Then he put the jar back between the rocks and went home to his mother.

When he got home he showed his mother what he had collected. "I got this from the lizard who bought the skin," he said. "Nobody else was at home, or else they ran when they saw me coming."

His mother said, "Where did you say the lizard keeps his money?"

He took her to the place and showed her the jar of gold. Now his mother knew that her son could never be expected to keep a secret. And if word got out that they had found this money, trouble might come looking for them. So she put her ear to the crack in the rocks and listened for a moment. "What's that again?" she asked, then listened some more. Then she turned to her son and said, "This is a very generous lizard. He's decided to pay us the price of the entire cow, for the sake of all those people who couldn't afford to pay."

She picked up the jar and put it under her robe, saying, "Now we have to hurry home. It looks like soon it's going to be raining yogurt."

When they got home she told her son to stand under the smoke hole of the roof with his mouth open to catch the falling yogurt. Then she went up on the roof with a gallon jar of yogurt. "Are you ready?" she called. "Here comes the rain!" And she poured the yogurt through the smoke hole into her son's mouth, and all over his face and clothes.

"Now," she said when she'd gotten him cleaned up. "If anyone should ask you where you got the gold, just tell them that the lizard gave it to you on the day it rained yogurt."

She made him repeat that back to her so she knew he remembered. The next day she sent him to town to buy food. As he took out the gold coins, he said to the merchant, "We got this from the lizard."

"Oh yeah," said the merchant. "What lizard?"

"The lizard by so-and-so's field."

"And when did you say this happened?"

"The day it rained yogurt."

"That's nice, kid. Get out of here."

No one ever inquired any further.

Now the house where the boy and his mother lived was right next door to a mosque. Five times a day the muezzin gave the call to prayer from the top of the mosque, and all the people stopped whatever they were doing to pray with him—all except this boy, who was exceedingly fond of sleep. At least three times a day the call to prayer cut him off in the middle of a nap, and when it did he would shout out the window, "Shut up or I'll throw you down from there!"

Of course it was the muezzin's sacred duty to make the prayers as the Holy Book commands. So he didn't stop. And one day as he finished the morning prayer, he met the boy coming up the steps of the minaret with a determined look on his face. "I told you to shut up or I'd throw you down from here," he said. And he grabbed the holy man and threw him over the rail.

When the boy came down from the minaret, there was the muezzin's body at the bottom. He wondered what he should do with it. "I'll take it to my mother," he thought. "She'll think of something."

"Come with me," said the mother. "We'll bury him together." The two of them dug a hole behind their house and buried the muezzin there. Then the boy went back in the house to take a nap. But when he was asleep, the mother killed a billy goat and cut off its head. She dug down into the hole where the muezzin was buried, and she placed the billy goat's head right over the head of the holy man. Then she covered it all over again.

That afternoon the foolish boy was lounging around in the market place when the muezzin's sons came looking for their father. When the boy heard their questions, he spoke right up. "You mean the guy who makes all that noise at the top of the mosque?"

"That's right. Have you seen him?"

"Seen him? I killed him."

"You what?"

"Killed him. Threw him off the top of the mosque. I told him I would for making all that racket, but I guess he didn't believe me."

The muezzin's sons didn't believe him either, but he said, "I'll show you where he's buried. My mother and I buried him in the backyard just this morning."

So they all went to the boy's house, and he began to dig at the spot where they'd buried the muezzin. After a while the spade struck something hard. He lowered himself into the dark grave and began to dig around with his hands. Finally he found something and gave a tug. What came up was the head of the billy goat.

"Does your father have horns on his head?" he asked the muezzin's sons.

"This boy is a lunatic," they said to themselves. "It's our fault for wasting our time with him." They went away to look for their father, and they never bothered the fool or his mother again.

—Yemen (Roosevelt)

The Young Man Who Made a Fortune From a Grain of Corn

Once upon a time there was a young man who lived alone with his mother. One day he said to his mother, "Give me a grain of corn and I'll go seek my fortune." So his mother gave him a grain of corn and he set out to seek his fortune.

He came to the next valley where he saw a woman tending a garden. "I'm hungry," he told the woman. "Will you cook my grain of corn for me?"

The woman thought he was a fool, but she agreed to cook his grain of corn. She put it in a pan with oil, but she forgot to watch it, and the grain of corn popped and jumped out the window, where a rooster stepped up and ate it.

"I want my grain of corn or the rooster that ate it," he told the woman. She didn't know what to do, so she gave him the rooster, and he went on seeking his fortune.

He came to the next valley and asked for a place to spend the night. The people brought him to a house where there were hens in one pen and camels in another. "You can leave your rooster in there with the hens," they told him.

"Oh no," he said, "Not this rooster. This rooster doesn't sleep with hens. He only sleeps with camels."

They thought he was an idiot, but they put his rooster in the pen with the camels and they all went to sleep.

In the morning he came out and found his rooster trampled to death, and he set up a terrible cry. "I want my rooster or the beast that stepped on him," he said to the people. They felt sorry for him, so they gave him a camel. He got up on the camel and set off for home, saying to himself, "This may not be a fortune, but its not bad."

He was almost home when he met a man dragging the body of his mother along the road. "Give her to me," he said, "and I will take care of her for you." Together they lifted the dead mother up on the back of the camel. Our hero went on down the road with the stranger's dead mother riding behind him.

He came to a wedding party, and he said to the bridegroom, "My old mother is sick. Could I sit her down under the canopy next to your wife?"

The groom said, "Sure."

They went on with the wedding, but when the bride got up to say the vows she jostled the old woman and she fell over. The young man began to cry. "My mother is dead! I want my mother or the woman who killed her!"

So they gave him the bride and all her property in place of the dead mother, and now he had his entire fortune. He took it all home to his own mother, who thanks be to Allah was still alive, and they all lived happily ever after.

—Yemen (Roosevelt)

The Daughter Whose Stomach Got Big

Once upon a time there was a daughter whose mother had died, and her father remarried. Her stepmother and two stepsisters didn't like this girl because her father loved her so much.

One day they prepared a special dish, just for her. Soon after she ate the food, her stomach began to swell. Day after day, her stomach got bigger and bigger.

After a while the stepmother went to the girl's father and said, "Your daughter is bad. Look at her. She's been with a man and she's pregnant."

Her father was furious. He went to his daughter and said, "Come with me. We are going on a long journey."

They walked toward the mountains for many days. Every night they lay down to sleep, and in the morning they got up to walk some more. At last they came to the mountains. They began to climb, but darkness fell, and they lay down to sleep on a high, flat rock.

After midnight, the father arose and slipped quietly away, leaving his daughter alone to die.

When the daughter awoke, she called to her father. But no one answered. She sat and wept, loudly and bitterly bewailing her fate.

But it so happened that a local prince was out riding, and he heard her cries. When he saw the girl he was touched by her beauty and her sadness, and he asked about her troubles. She told him that her father had brought her here and left her to die.

"Why?" asked the prince. But she only shook her head as if she didn't know.

Then the prince noticed that although her face was thin and drawn, her stomach was big and swollen. He asked her why.

She said she didn't know. He said, "Think hard."

She thought hard, but she couldn't remember.

"When did it start?" he asked.

Then she remembered the special dish her stepmother gave her. When she told the prince the story, he knew what to do. He took her to a place where wild garlic grew, and gave her plenty of garlic to chew and swallow. Then he made her wash it down with lots and lots of fresh water. When she got tired he made her drink some more. Suddenly she felt as if she was going to be sick. Her stomach heaved, and out of her mouth came a great big, fat, snake.

Everything the girl had eaten since the day she ate her stepmother's special dish had gone not to her, but into the belly of the snake. It fell out on the ground and the prince cut it in half. Then the girl fell down, nearly dead herself. Not only was her stomach no longer big—she was as skinny as a starving child.

The prince took her home and nursed her back to health, fell in love with her, and married her—of course. And so they lived there happily together; she bore him many healthy children, and never another snake.

—Yemen (Roosevelt)

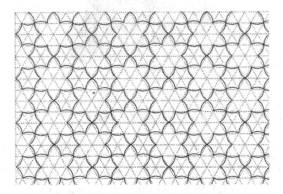

AFRICA

The Lazy Donkey

Once upon a time there was a donkey who went out with her friend Cow to find something to eat. They went into the jungle and found a beautiful field of tasty grass, and they both started eating.

Donkey ate so much grass that she started getting happy. She reared back and said to Cow, "I'm gonna bray!"

Cow said, "Don't do that! If you bray once, you'll let Hyena know where we are."

But Donkey was ready to burst. She said, "I don't care! I've gotta bray!" And she reared back and let loose: "HEEEEE-HAAAAWWWW!"

Cow was angry. She said, "Now Hyena knows we're out here. You bray once more and he'll come after us."

They ate a while longer until Donkey started getting happy again. She said, "I—I—I—I—I'm gonna bray!"

Cow said, "Don't do it! Hyena will come after us!"

"I don't care! I've just gotta bray!" And she let one rip. "HEEEEEE-HAAAAWWWW!"

Cow said, "I'm getting out of here. If you bray one more time, Hyena will find you and eat your big fat happy behind." And Cow took off for home at a fast trot.

Now Donkey was sorry to see her friend leaving. But she was still a little hungry so she went right back to eating that sweet green grass. And it wasn't long before she felt herself getting happy again. "I—I—I—I—I'm gonna bray!" she cried. And there was nobody around to even try and stop her. So she reared back and let it rip: "HEEEEE-HAAAAAWWWWWW!"

Before she was finished, Hyena jumped out of the jungle onto Donkey's back, bit her on the neck, and killed her.

Hyena ate for a while on Donkey's tender parts, and then he called for his servant, Dog. "Cut this creature up for me for later," he told Dog. "Eat your fill, but be sure to save me the brain." Hyena had a special fondness for Donkey brain. It was a great hyena delicacy.

So Dog set to work cutting up Donkey for later. All the while he'd taste the pieces—a little flank, a little thigh, a little liver, a little throat—until he chewed open Donkey's skull and there it was—the brain.

Dog said to himself, "Surely it wouldn't hurt to try just a little taste of this, as I've tasted everything else on this delicious beast." So Dog reached in and took just a nibble of brain. It was so good! Dog had never tasted anything quite so intoxicatingly sweet, juicy, soft, and nourishing. And before he knew what he was doing, he'd eaten every bit.

When Dog realized what he had done, he sat up and looked around. Hyena was relaxing in the shade.

Better think, Dog thought.

Dog barked a couple times to wake Hyena. Hyena got up and ambled over to Donkey's carcass. "Finished?" he asked Dog.

"Yep," Dog said.

Hyena poked his snout into Donkey's skull. "Hey!" he barked. "Didn't I tell you to save me the brain?" He took a couple of menacing steps toward Dog.

"I know you told me save you the brain," Dog said, "But this Donkey didn't have a brain."

"He didn't have a brain? What are you talking about?"

"If she'd had a brain, would she have stood here braying till you came and killed her?"

Hyena had to admit that Dog was right. And the moral of the story is: If you have a brain, you can get yourself out of trouble—but you can also keep yourself out of trouble in the first place.

—Ethiopia (Senn)

Hyena and Fox

Once upon a time Fox went hunting and left her kits home in the den by themselves. Hyena came and knocked on the door. He disguised his voice to sound like the kit's mother, and he said, "Children, children, open the door. I've caught some delicious morsels to cook for our dinner." But when the little foxes opened the door, Hyena grabbed them and knocked their heads together and cooked them and ate them all up.

When Fox came home she saw the open door and a dirty pot, but her children were gone. She went out looking for them. She looked and looked.

She met Rabbit and asked, "Rabbit, oh, Rabbit, have you seen my children?" Rabbit said no.

She met Tortoise. "Tortoise, oh, Tortoise, have you seen my children?" Tortoise said no.

She met Tiger. "Tiger, oh, Tiger, have you seen my children?" Tiger said no, but Fox had better run or he'd eat her too.

So she ran till she met Lion. "Lion, oh, Lion, have you seen my children?"

Lion was King of Beasts and had lots of animals telling him news. He said, "I've heard that Mr. Hyena cooked them in your own pot and ate them for his dinner."

Now Fox wanted just one thing: revenge. She invited Hyena to dinner. Under Hyena's chair she dug a pit and filled it full of fire. When Hyena sat down, she fell in the pit, and Fox quickly covered it over with mats and branches.

"Fox, my dear friend, let me out of this pit."

"Burn, burn, like you burned my kits."

And that was the end of Hyena, that time.

—Eritrea (Senn)

The Three Servants

Once upon a time there was a king. He lived in a big house with beautiful gardens, but he was lonely because he didn't have a wife.

In the king's house there were three maidservants. One day when the king was walking in his garden, he heard the three servants talking there together, and he hid behind a bush to listen.

One of the maidservants said, "Let's play 'I wish.'" They all agreed to tell each other a wish.

The first girl said, "I wish I was married to the king."

The second girl said, "Oh no, that's much too big a wish. I wish I was the king's wife's hair-dresser."

The third girl said, "I wish I was his children's nursemaid."

The king stepped out from his hiding place and said, "I will make your wishes come true. You," he told the first girl, "will be my wife. And you," the second girl, "will be my wife's hair-dresser. And you," he told the third girl, "will look after our children when they are born."

So the king took his new bride-to-be into the palace and they were married.

The second and third maidservants, though, were not happy to see their old friend married to the king. In the silence of the night they complained to each other, "Why did she get to marry the king? Is she any better than you or me? No! It's just pure dumb luck, that's all." And they burned with envy.

When it came time for them to help deliver the queen's first baby, they agreed to hide the child and tell the king it was born dead. And when the time came they were able to steal the baby away and hide it in a basket in the closet of their room.

But when they told the king that his son was dead he went mad with grief and demanded to see the body. They told him, "We've already disposed of the body in the river."

The king had a feeling that something was wrong. So he locked the two wicked maidservants in their room and had his menservants search the river for the body. The maidservants panicked and threw the basket with the baby in it out their window into the river. There it was found by the men searching along the bank. The baby in the basket was healthy and unharmed.

The king and his wife were overjoyed to have their baby back. The two maidservants were put into prison, while the king and the maidservant who had become his queen lived happily ever after and had many more children.

—Ethiopia (Senn)

In Ethiopia not too long ago there lived a man named Alaqa Giibri-Hanna. There are many stories told about him. Here is one.

Alaqa Giibri-Hanna

Once there was a rich man in the neighborhood who was getting married. Everyone was invited to the wedding feast except for Alaqa Giibri-Hanna and a neighbor woman with a bad reputation.

On the wedding day they put up an enormous tent, and all the people were eating and drinking and making merry. Alaqa Giibri-Hanna went to the neighbor woman who hadn't been invited, and he said, "You want to go to the feast? I have a plan. I'll take this stick, and I'll pretend to beat you with it. I'll chase you into the tent, and once we're inside they'll have to invite us to eat."

She agreed. So Alaqa Giibri-Hanna took his stick and raised it against the woman. She screamed and took off in the direction of the wedding tent. Every time he swung the stick at her she screamed, "Help! He's killing me!" Till they crashed through the door of the tent.

"Iniquitous witch! Take that!"

"Help! People! Alaqa Giibri-Hanna is going to kill me!"

The respectable men of the gathering stepped between them. "Now, now, neighbors, we mustn't carry on so at a wedding feast. It's bad luck. Won't you sit down here with us and eat. Full mouths can speak no evil."

Alaqa Giibri-Hanna glared at the neighbor woman, then suddenly smiled. "Alright neighbors, if you insist, we will honor this feast with our presence."

So they seated Alaqa Giibri-Hanna and the neighbor woman at one of the big communal tables. There was a gigantic flatbread, known as *injera,* spread across the table in the traditional Ethiopian style, with big helpings of food upon it. Across the table from Alaqa Giibri-Hanna was a huge lamb shank, dripping with grease. Alaqa Giibri-Hanna's mouth began to water just looking at it. But it's considered very bad manners in Ethiopia to reach across someone's place to pick up food. So instead, Alaqa Giibri-Hanna began to shout at his neighbor, "Wicked hag, I'm not through with you yet! Just wait till I get you outside!"

"Shut your ugly face, you old goat!"

"That's it! I'll show you!" And he reached across her place, picked up the lamb shank, and raised it over his head as if to brain her with it. The respectable neighbors leaped up. "No, no, no, no, no!" they cried. "That is not for hitting! That's for eating!"

Alaqa Giibri-Hanna glared at the woman, then smiled, and slowly lowered the lamb shank. "Ah, yes. Of course, you are right. It's for eating." And he solemnly sat down, raised the meat to his lips, and ate every last bit of it.

—Ethiopia (Senn)

Once upon a time there was a very timid man by the name of Egal Shidaad. In some ways he resembles Nasruddin. There are many stories told about him in Somalia. Here is one.

Egal Shidaad

One day some men came to see Egal Shidaad about a debt. As they approached his house he told his wife, "Hide me! Cover me with grass so they think I'm not at home."

They came. They asked, "Where is Egal Shidaad?"

His wife said, "I don't know. He is not at home."

"Where is he?"

"I don't know," she said.

"When will he be back?"

"I don't know."

"You don't know much about your husband, do you?"

"I don't know."

"How long has he been missing?"

Egal Shidaad was listening under his covering of grass. He was embarrassed that his wife seemed ignorant in front of his creditors, so he finally called out from his burial place, "Two or three days."

They said, "What was that?"

"I said, two or three days," said Egal Shidaad's wife. "He has been gone two or three days."

"But who was that calling out?"

"That was no one."

The creditors started to leave. As they were going, Egal Shidaad's wife whispered, "What do you mean, calling out like that? I told them that you weren't here. You made me look like a fool."

Egal Shidaad said, "You were already looking like a fool. I was only trying to help."

"If I need your help I'll ask for it."

The men heard two voices arguing. They turned around and came back. "Who is that you are arguing with? Where is Egal Shidaad?"

Egal Shidaad's wife stared at them. Finally she said, "He is dead."

"Dead?"

"Yes." She started to cry. "He died yesterday. I buried him here. Poor man. I still like to argue with him, for old time's sake." She blew her nose loudly and cried, "Oh my dear husband, why did you leave me alone?" And she gave the grass mound a vicious kick.

The creditors were ashamed. They offered their sympathy to the grieving widow and they went away.

—Somalia (Roosevelt)

The Dancing Tree

One time during market days, Tortoise had no money and nothing to sell. But he still wanted some of the food that the people had brought to market.

So he dug a tunnel under the marketplace up to the roots of the giant tree that stood on the edge of the marketplace. And with his great strength he took hold of the roots of the giant tree and started moving them up and down like rods of a giant puppet. Up above in the marketplace it looked like the tree was dancing.

When the people in the marketplace saw the dancing tree they were terrified. It looked like the tree was moving toward them to crush them. Perhaps it was a curse from the angry gods. Soon everyone in the marketplace was running away in terror. When the marketplace was empty, Tortoise came up from his tunnel and took what he wanted from people's goods.

The next day people were back in the marketplace selling their goods. The tree began to dance again. It actually seemed to be moving from its place and coming toward them (it was Tortoise moving the roots from underneath in his tunnel). Again they ran away in terror. And again Tortoise came up and ate his fill.

This happened the next day the same way. Now, as well as being frightened, the people were worried that their goods were disappearing. They went to the king for advice and protection. The king said, "Let me see this strange sight for myself. I'll show you that it is nothing to fear."

The king went to the marketplace and waited with the people. At the usual time the tree began to dance. The king felt fear but he tried not to show it. "This is strange," he said. "But surely the dancing tree can't hurt us."

Just then the tree began to move from its place, coming toward the people. The king was the first one out of the marketplace. He ran so fast that his crown fell off his head and bounced along the ground. Tortoise came up and ate his fill.

Now since the king couldn't help them, the people went to a *babalao* (a priest of the Yoruba God Ogun), a powerful man who could cast spells and uncover secrets. The *babalao* said that he could make no guarantees, but that he could make something that might help them get to the bottom of this.

He made a statue, an image of a man, and set it up in the marketplace. The next day when the tree began to dance, everybody ran away but the statue still stood there.

When Tortoise came up to get what he wanted from people's goods, he saw the statue standing there. "Hey," he said. "Who are you? What are you doing here?" The statue didn't answer.

"Hey, I said, what are you doing here? Didn't you see the dancing tree?"

No answer.

Tortoise said, "Dancing tree's gonna get you. Crush you. Eat you." Statue didn't even blink. "Hey!" Tortoise said. "Don't you hear me?" Statue didn't answer. "I'M TALKING TO YOU! SAY SOMETHING OR I'LL PUNCH YOU!"

Statue didn't say anything. So Tortoise reared back and punched the statue, but the *babalao* had put a spell on the statue so that Tortoise's hand stuck to it.

"Let me go!" he said. "Let me go or I'll punch you with my other hand!" The statue didn't let him go, and it didn't say anything. So Tortoise reared back and punched it with his other hand. It too stuck fast.

"I said, LET ME GO!" Tortoise screamed. "Let me go or I'll kick you!" The statue didn't let go, so Tortoise kicked it. Now his foot was stuck.

"Let me go or I'll kick you with my other foot!" The statue didn't let go, of course, and soon Tortoise was stuck fast to the statue with all four feet.

Now the people came out and surrounded Tortoise and took him before the king.

Tortoise was sentenced to be whipped thirty stripes every day for the whole month. And since then Tortoise never uses his great strength to scare the people or steal from them.

—Nigeria (Senn)

Yams for the Taking

There was a terrible famine in Tortoise's country, and his family was starving. So Tortoise went to his old partner, Dog, and said, "Dog old friend, let's go traveling and see if we can track down some food for our families."

So Tortoise and Dog went walking and walking till they came to a land of plenty. There was a farmer in that country who had so many ripe yams that he left them in a great big pile till he could come back later and take them to the market. Dog and Tortoise came upon the mountain of yams and they were astonished.

"What kind of country is this?" said Tortoise. "Here are hundreds of yams, right here for the taking!"

Dog said, "It is certainly a wonderful country. But are you sure these were left here for the taking?"

"What else could they be sitting here for?"

"Perhaps they are here for the selling and the seller has gone away for a minute. Or perhaps it is some kind of test they give to strangers."

"Nonsense," said Tortoise, who was thinking entirely with his stomach. "These yams are here for the taking, and I am going to take as many as I can carry. Isn't that what we came for?"

Dog had to admit that that was, indeed, what they came for. But he was still uneasy. He said,

"I'm just going to take a few and return home to my family. That's all I can carry home safely anyhow." And dog picked out just three of the ripest yams that he could easily carry in his arms.

But Tortoise wanted it all. He would have taken the whole pile if he could have devised the magic to do it. Instead he began to gather up yams by the dozens, till he could hardly see over them. Yams were falling and rolling in every direction. He started that way along the road for home.

Yams kept dropping out of the pile in his arms. Tortoise would try and catch them and other yams would fall out. He kept right on dropping and stopping, scooping and wrestling with those loose yams all over the road, and he hardly got anywhere at all.

Dog said, "I'd love to stay and help you, old friend, but I can hear my children's stomachs growling all the way from here." And Dog took off at a trot.

Soon the farmer came back to his field to take his yams to market. He noticed that the pile had gotten smaller. Then he noticed a trail of dropped yams leading down the road toward Tortoise's country. The farmer didn't have to follow it far before he caught up with Tortoise.

"Villain, what are you doing with my crop?"

"Pardon me sir, I'm a stranger here," said Tortoise. "In my country we only make piles of food like that when we mean to give it away."

But Tortoise was taken in front of a judge, who didn't buy that story. Instead, Tortoise was condemned to be the slowest of all the animals, so he can never again hope to get away with more than he can carry.

And that was that.

—Nigeria (Senn)

How Tortoise Broke His Shell

Once upon a time the King of the Birds sent out a grand invitation to the birds of the world. There would be a great feast in heaven for all the feathered creatures on the face of the earth. Tortoise was a close friend of Parrot, so he heard about the feast. And when he heard about it, he wanted to go.

Tortoise had no feathers, but he was very clever and very persuasive. With Parrot's help he got each bird to lend him one feather, and when he wove all those feathers together to make a coat, he was more colorful than any of the birds—even more colorful than Parrot. And now Tortoise could go to the feast.

On the appointed day, Tortoise showed up at the gathering place wearing his coat of feathers. He told the birds, "For today I will have a different name. Because my coat has feathers from all of you, my bird name will be 'All-of-you.'" The birds applauded him for this nice compliment.

When they reached the court of the King of the Birds, each bird had to introduce himself and give his name—"I am Eagle," "I am Hawk," "I am Heron," "I am Sparrow," and so on. When it was Tortoise's turn he said grandly, "I am All-of-you."

All the birds applauded and cried out their approval. Then the king ordered his waiters to bring in the first course of food and wine.

"This is for all of you," they announced.

"That's me!" cried Tortoise. "This course is for me!" And before anyone could think of an argument, Tortoise ate all the food and drank all the wine.

The second course was brought, and again the waiters announced, "This is for all of you."

"Me again," cried Tortoise, and he ate up the entire second course.

A third time the waiters brought out delicate food and wines and proclaimed, "This is for all of you," and a third time Tortoise claimed it for himself. Now the birds were angry. They decided to take their feathers back from Tortoise's coat—all of them.

"Now let's see how well you fly home, with all our food in your belly and no feathers on your back."

"Parrot, old friend," said Tortoise. "Won't you go down and tell my wife to put out all the mattresses and pillows and every soft thing she can find to cushion my fall?"

"Certainly, my old friend, I'll talk to your wife," said Parrot. So Parrot flew down to call on Tortoise's wife. But Parrot was just as mad at Tortoise as the rest of the birds—maybe madder, because he had thought Tortoise was his friend. So he said to Tortoise's wife, "Tortoise wants you to put out all the hardest, sharpest objects you can find—sharp stones, axes, machetes, broken bottles, everything. He wants to see how softly he can land with his new coat of feathers."

"That Tortoise is crazy," said his wife. But she did as she thought her husband wanted.

Parrot flew back up to heaven and said, "Your landing spot is ready." And Tortoise jumped. He landed on the stones and axes and broken bottles. His shell, which once was as smooth and round as a crystal ball, shattered into hundreds of jagged pieces. The birds flew over and jeered at him. Tortoise couldn't move because of his broken back.

Ant came walking by and saw Tortoise lying there. He asked what had happened, and when he heard, he took pity on Tortoise (the birds were no friends of Ant's, anyhow). Ant went and gathered the broken pieces of Tortoise's shell and stuck them back together. But he couldn't get them back in perfect order.

So when Tortoise finally healed there were jagged scars around all the broken pieces of his shell. He was never as handsome, or as clever, or as tricky, or as hungry, or as quick as he was when he went to the feast in heaven at the palace of the King of the Birds and his name was "All-of-you."

—Nigeria (Senn)

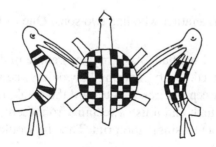

Why Tortoise's Head Is Bald

In olden times, Tortoise was considered one of the handsomest animals in the jungle because of his beautiful, thick, curly head of hair. One day he was invited to a feast at the home of the king and queen, Lion and Lioness. Tortoise spent all morning washing and combing and curling and brushing his hair. Then he put on his hat and went off to the feast.

When he got there, many kinds of food were laid out for the taking. Tortoise looked high and low for his favorite food—porridge—but he couldn't find it anywhere. The king and queen went outside at some point, leaving Tortoise alone in the dining room. And then he smelled that special smell coming out of the kitchen—*porridge*.

Tortoise snuck into the kitchen and took a little taste. Oh, it was hot! But it was so good. He had to have some. But he had nothing to put it in. Then he thought of his hat. He was so hungry for porridge that he took off his hat and quickly filled it up with the steaming, sticky stuff. Then he heard the voices of Lion and Lioness coming into the house. He was caught! Without even thinking, Tortoise whipped his hat back onto his head and rushed back into the dining room.

"Tortoise! The guests are arriving! Are you ready for the feast?"

"King, I'm not feeling well at all. I need to go home and take a steambath."

"Stay a while longer. We haven't even brought out the porridge!"

"My apologies, King, but I really must be off."

Lioness noticed oil from the porridge leaking down from under Tortoise's hat, and she said, "Tortoise, what is that sticky stuff dripping down your forehead?"

Tortoise said, "It's sweat. I must be getting a fever."

Lion said, "Tortoise, remove your hat in the presence of your King." And now Tortoise had to remove his hat—and when he did, all the boiling hot porridge rolled down his face and neck and into the collar of his shell. He put his hands up to wipe it off and his hands got burned too. All the guests roared with laughter to see that Tortoise had taken food without asking while it was cooking and then had gotten burned for it.

Tortoise was sent home from the feast, never to be asked back. But what was worse, his beautiful, thick, curly hair and his eyebrows and eyelashes were all burned off. To this day, Tortoise's head and hands are hairless and wrinkled, like one who has been burned. And he isn't very handsome anymore.

And now you know why.

—Nigeria (Senn)

The Dwarf Baby

A long time ago there was a father who had two sons. One of the sons was considered smart, the other was not.

The smart one worked hard and had lots of money. People in the village thought the other son was the laziest boy who ever lived. Every morning he would sweep the ground under a big tree in his father's compound. He'd sweep in circles, in toward the trunk, and when he reached the center he would climb up on the first limb and finish sweeping from there, so that the ground beneath the tree was perfectly smooth, without a single footprint. Then he would spend the afternoons sleeping in the shady branches of the tree.

One day their mother went to her fields to work. And that day, under a banana tree, she found a baby dwarf, a kind of goblin called an *abwatiea* in the Twi language. "What a cute one," she thought. "If I take him home and clean him up a little, he'll be an adorable little baby." So she took him home.

Now *abwatiea* babies have long hair, not just on their heads, but growing all over their backs. The mother cut the dwarf's hair on top, and then she took a razor and shaved its back. "Now," she said, "he's a real nice little boy."

That evening the *abwatiea's* mother and father went looking for their baby. They looked under the banana tree, and when they didn't find him there they kept looking till they got to the human family's house.

The human mother had just finished putting away the supper dishes when she turned around and saw the dwarf mother and father standing by the baby's bed.

"What have you done to our baby?" they demanded.

"I—I—I just tried to clean him up a little," she said.

"You've ruined him," they said. "You put the hair you stole from him back on our baby by tomorrow morning, or we'll take you with us as our slave." And they disappeared.

As it happened, the mother had burned the dwarf baby's hair in the fire, so now she was in big trouble. She called her smart, rich, industrious son. But he didn't know what to do. He just yelled at her for doing such a stupid thing. The lazy son heard them yelling and crying and carrying on, and he came down from his tree to find out what was the matter. "You can't help," they told him. "You're too lazy and dumb." But he insisted on knowing the trouble, and they finally told him.

He said, "Just leave it to me." And he went to sleep.

Next morning when the *abwatieas* came back to claim their own, the lazy son was there to meet them. "You want my mother to put the hair that she cut back on your baby or you'll take her as a slave," he said. "But let's see you sweep the ground underneath my tree and leave no footprints anywhere. If you can do that, then you can take my mother. If you can't, you can just take your baby and go away."

The dwarves agreed to try, but every place they swept they left footprints somewhere else. They tried sweeping on tiptoes, on one foot, even jumping up and down, but they always made a mess somewhere. *Abwatieas* can't climb trees like the lazy son could. So finally they had to take their shaved baby and go away.

And the mother and the whole village learned that everybody has their place, and that the one who looks lazy may just be waiting for his chance to serve.

—Ghana (Senn)

The Magic Cane

A long time ago there was a father who lived alone with his two sons. One year there was a draught, and they had no food. The father went to the fields to try to find something for his children to eat.

At the far end of his fields he found a cane. But it was no ordinary cane. It was covered from top to bottom with delicately colored designs.

"What cane is so beautiful as this?" cried the father.

Then the cane spoke. It said, "I am not so beautiful. But if you want something to eat, just say the word."

"What word?" asked the father.

"How about, 'Produce.' "

The father said "Produce," and suddenly the ground around the cane was covered with melons, yams, and all kinds of vegetables and fruits.

"I like this!" said the father.

"There's more," said the cane.

"More? Like what?"

"Why don't you see what happens when you say, 'Whip me'?"

The father was enjoying himself so much with this magic cane that he said to himself, "Why not?" And out loud he said, "Whip me."

The cane rose up and began to whip him all over. The father yelled, "OW! OW! OW! OW!" with every blow. Just then a bird flew over and the father distinctly heard it say, "If you weren't such a fool you'd just say, 'STOP!' "

So he did—he yelled, "STOP!" And the cane stopped and laid itself peacefully down at the father's feet.

I will take this home to feed my children, the father thought. So he took the magic cane and hid it in the shed next to their house. Every time they needed food, the father would go there, take the cane, and say, "Produce." And they had plenty of food all through the winter.

The younger son began to wonder where all their food was coming from because all the other families were suffering from the draught. One day he followed his father to the shed, and he saw him take the cain in his hands and say, "Produce." And there was food.

The next day, when his father had gone to the fields, the younger son went to the shed and took out the cane. He was enchanted with its beauty. "What cane is so beautiful as this?" he said.

"I am not so beautiful," said the cane. "But if you want something to eat, just say the word."

"What word?"

"How about, 'Produce'?"

So the son said "Produce," and there were all kinds of vegetables and fruits in the shed. The son began to eat.

When he was done, the cane said, "Do you want to see what happens when you say, 'Whip me'?"

So the son said, "Whip me." The cane began to whip him all over. "OW! OW! OW! OW!" the boy shouted. Then he grabbed ahold of the cane and broke it over his knee. The cane disappeared.

That evening when the father came home, he went to the shed to get food from the magic cane. But it was gone.

He went to his sons. "Did you take something from the shed," he asked them. They wouldn't say. Then he saw that the younger son had bruises and scrapes on his body, as if he had been whipped. And he knew.

"All you had to say was 'Stop!' " he told his son.

But it was too late. There was no more free food after that.

—Ghana (Senn)

The Two Brothers

Mr. and Mrs. Addo had been long without a child. They decided to visit a fetish priest to ask for help. The priest gave them some root medicine. They used the medicine for several days and Mrs. Addo became pregnant. In time she gave birth to twins, brothers named Panin and Kakra.

The two boys grew up handsome and tall. One day they decided to go to the forest to see which of them could bring back the most beautiful flower. Panin, who was the first born, told Kakra to look in the thicket while he looked in the meadow. They would meet in an hour at the edge of the village yam fields.

So Kakra went into the thicket and Panin went into the meadow. But when they came to the meeting place, Kakra had a flower that shone like a star. It made Panin's flower look ill. Panin was seized with jealousy. He killed his brother and took the beautiful flower. When Panin came home, his mother asked him where Kakra was. He said he didn't know—he just set the beautiful flower down on the windowsill and sat staring at it.

They sent word to the local chief that Kakra was missing. The villagers searched high and low, but they didn't find the younger twin. One day, Mrs. Addo went to the fields to dig for yams. As she dug, her knife hit a bone, and the bone began to sing:

"Hit me again, hit me again, my mother.
Panin my brother took my beautiful flower,
And left me here in the cold, cold ground.
So hit me again."

Mrs. Addo dug up the bones of her son. She took them to the palace of the chief. When the chief came in, she struck them with her knife, and again the bones began to sing:

"Hit me again, hit me again, my mother.
Panin my brother took my beautiful flower,
And left me here in the cold cold ground,
So hit me again."

So they called for Panin. "What have you done with your brother Kakra?" they asked him.

"I have done nothing."

"Do you know whose bones these are?"

"I don't know them."

"But they know you." The mother struck the bones with her knife, and the bones began to sing:

"Hit me again, hit me again, my mother.
Panin my brother took my beautiful flower,
And left me here in the cold cold ground,
So hit me again."

They took Panin to the river and threw him in. He whirled in the current and sank from sight, and the villagers never saw him again.

—Ghana (Senn)

Anansi the Spider

Anansi the Spider had a big family, and they had a very big farm.

Anansi's family was so big that even though his farm produced a lot of food, Anansi never got to eat as much of it as he wanted. Anansi thought that if he could live out in the fields instead of in the village with his family, then he would get first crack at all the freshest, ripest, tastiest food.

So one day when his wife came to wake him, she found Anansi lying in bed with his arms and legs sticking straight up in the air. "*Aieeee!*" she screamed. "Anansi is dead!"

All the family came running. "He sure looks dead," they agreed.

Some of the nephews and nieces tried poking him but he didn't move. "Stop that," said the grownups. "It's not nice."

So they started making funeral arrangements. While they were weeping and wailing and arguing and so forth, a strange voice suddenly broke in: "Don't bury Anansi in the village graveyard," it said.

It was Anansi talking. But they didn't call him Anansi the Trickster for nothing. He was able to throw his voice, so it looked to everybody in the room as if a spirit was talking. Everybody got very quiet. "It's Anansi's ghost," they whispered. "Or maybe his guardian spirit!"

"If not in the graveyard," they asked the spirit, "then where?"

"Take Anansi's body to the fields. His spirit would like to rest on the farm that he loved so much. And don't put him beneath the ground. Put up a tent on the edge of the best field of yams, and lay him on a soft platform bed, so his spirit can look over the beautiful fields for all eternity."

It made sense to the family. They put up a tent on the edge of Anansi's favorite field, and they laid Anansi's body down on his favorite bed. The spirit voice kept breaking in and giving directions whenever they forgot the wishes of the deceased.

After a most touching funeral celebration, they all went back to their homes in the village. Then Anansi got up, flexed his arms and legs, and went to work digging, picking, and eating all the freshest, ripest, tastiest vegetables and fruits that he could find by moonlight.

"Being dead really gives a fellow an appetite," he said.

After a while the family began to notice that somebody or something was eating their best produce. But they could never catch the thief. Meanwhile, Anansi's corpse kept getting fatter and fatter. But nobody noticed that.

One day, to catch the thief, Anansi's children made a statue of a man. They covered the statue with glue, left it in the fields, and went home.

When Anansi came out for his night of feeding, he met the statue. He thought it was there to steal his food. "Who are you," he demanded. "What are you doing on my farm?"

The statue didn't answer. "You think I'm a fool, that I can talk and you won't answer me? Talk to me or I'll hit you. This is my farm!" Still the statue didn't answer. So Anansi hit it with his fist. And his hand stuck tight to the glue. Anansi hit the statue with his other hand and his feet in turn. Soon he was stuck to the statue with all eight limbs.

When Anansi's family came to the farm in the morning, they were surprised to see that their little trap had caught the spider himself. "Now you can really overlook your farm land for all eternity," they said. And they left Anansi hanging from the statue.

Maybe he's hanging there still.

—Ghana (Senn)

ASIA

The Four Wishes

Once upon a time there was a fisherman—an excellent fisherman—whose name was Don Juan. He lived alone with his wife and his dog Blackie. One day, when Don Juan was fishing on the sea, he saw something floating and he grabbed it with his net. It was a beautiful old-fashioned bottle.

Don Juan said to himself, "This is something worth keeping." As soon as he got to shore he opened the stopper on the bottle to see what might be inside. Imagine his surprise when a cloud of black smoke began pouring out of the bottle and gathered into a cloud the shape of a man. It was a genie. "Thank you for freeing me," the genie said. "Long ago a witch defeated me in battle and put me inside this bottle and threw me into the sea. I've been floating this way for a thousand years till you found me and set me free. You are my master. Ask now, and I will grant you four wishes."

"Ummm," said Don Juan, "I never thought about any wishes. What do you think I should ask?"

"That's up to you," said the genie.

"Oh gosh," said Don Juan. "How 'bout a fish? A real big fish."

There in the boat lay a tuna, with its head and tail poking over the bow and stern. "That's a nice big fish," said Juan. He cut off a piece and cooked it right there and ate it.

"What about your other three wishes?" asked the genie.

"Can't think now. Gotta get the rest of this home to the wife." The genie told Don Juan that he would wait by the shore in case he thought of something.

Then the fisherman took the rest of the tuna home to his wife. He told her about the genie and she began to think. She said, "Why don't we wish for a big house?"

"We already have a house," said Juan.

"This piece of junk you call a house? Go back to the genie, tell him we want a new house, nice and big—or else I'm outta here!"

The fisherman went down to the shore and called the genie. The genie appeared in a cloud of smoke, and asked, "Master—what is your wish?"

"My wife wants a new house, nice and big—or else she's outta there!"

"Your wish is granted," said the genie, and he disappeared.

When Don Juan got home, he saw his wife waving at him from a third-story window. "That's one nice, big house," he cried. They spent one happy night.

But in the morning, his wife was dissatisfied. "I think we've outgrown this place," she said. "And you can't get decent help around here. Go back to the genie. Tell him we want a palace, with plenty of servants."

"What do we need with a palace and servants? We just got into this nice, big house."

"Get going, you lazy slob—or I'm outta here!"

So Don Juan went down to the shore, and called the genie.

"What is my master's wish?"

"My wife wants a palace, with plenty of servants. She can't get along in that big house you gave us yesterday."

"Go home. Your wish is granted."

So the fisherman went home. There, where his nice big house had been, he found a palace rising to the sky, all made out of marble. His wife was in the Great Hall, seated on a marble throne, surrounded by servants. But when he came toward her throne, she looked at him with a terrible, dissatisfied frown. "I'm tired of this palace and all these stupid servants," she cried. "I want to be Queen of the Stars, the Moon, and the Sun."

Don Juan was shocked at his wife's request. "You can't be queen of all those things. There's only one God, and you're not Him!"

In the most terrible voice imaginable, his wife said that he had better do as she said and go ask the genie or she would have his head cut off and the pieces of him fed to his precious fish.

"Okay, okay, don't get steamed." So Don Juan went to the shore and called the genie.

"What is my master's fourth wish?"

"You're not gonna like this," Don Juan said. "My wife is tired of the palace already. She wants to be Queen of the Stars, the Moon, and the Sun."

The black smoke that the genie was made of began to swirl furiously. "Bad wish. Bad wish. There's only one God. Go home. Your wife has been punished for her sins."

The fisherman went home and found his wife sitting on a stepladder in front of their little old rickety house, muttering to herself. Don Juan realized that she had gone insane.

"I think I need a little time to myself," he said. He went back down to the shore and sat there looking at the waves.

Suddenly the genie came to him in a swirl of smoke. "Master, I will give you three more wishes. The last three you told me were not yours. They were your wife's. Now it is your turn."

"Oh, I'm no good at wishes," said the fisherman. He thought for a moment. "But I'm pretty hungry. How about a nice fat fish—all fried up already this time?"

"Deep fried, Master," said the genie graciously. And Don Juan had dinner. And the genie said to himself that he had found a kind and unselfish man for a master.

—Philippines, Tagalog (Mather)

Lazy Juan

This is a story about a young man named Lazy Juan. He doesn't like to work, so he finds other ways to do things.

Juan's mother sent him to town one day to run some errands. When he got to market he bought some fresh crabs for their dinner. He was too lazy to carry the wriggling creatures home. "We live on the water," he thought. "Why don't I just give them directions to our house and let them swim?" So he took them to the end of the dock and threw them in the water. Then he yelled out directions to his house and told the crabs to meet him there.

When Lazy Juan got home, his mother asked him what happened to the crabs. "I put them in the water and gave them directions to swim here." Juan saw the look on his mother's face. "You mean those stupid crabs aren't here yet?"

She went at him with the soup ladle. "Get out of here! If you can't do any better than that, you're not getting any dinner in this house!"

Lazy Juan got very hungry, and he had no money to buy food. Then he saw a guava tree covered with fruit. The fruit looked delicious, but Juan was too lazy to climb up and pick any. What he did instead was sit down under the tree, pick out a particularly ripe looking fruit above his head, and open his mouth, waiting for the fruit to fall into it.

As far as anybody knows, he's still waiting.

—Philippines (Roosevelt)

The Enchanted Adarna Bird

Once upon a time in a far away land there was a king who was dying of a mysterious illness. The king's most trusted adviser told the family that the only hope for his recovery was to let him hear the song of the enchanted Adarna bird. But in addition to having a song that could cure any illness of man, the Adarna bird lived at the end of the earth and had other magical powers that rendered it all but impossible to capture.

The king had three sons: the eldest Don Diego, the middle son Don Pedro, and the youngest, Juan, who was a fool. All three were determined to capture the Adarna bird and cure their father.

It was the eldest, Don Diego, who started first. He traveled by foot for many a weary mile. He passed through towns and villages and mountains and deserts, but he was brave and strong and never felt fear.

On his way through the desert he met an old broken down man who begged him for water. But Don Diego was cruel. He pushed the old man away, saying he only had enough for himself. On he went to the edge of the desert, till he came to the giant limestone mountain where the Adarna bird had its nest. He scaled the mountain, and at the top was a tree, and at the top of the tree was the enchanted Adarna bird, singing its sweet melodies. With every note the feathers of the enchanted bird changed color, from yellow to green to purple to red, to all the colors of the rainbow. Don Diego quietly approached the bird, but with every step his eyelids grew heavier. The sound and the sight of the bird was making him sleepier and sleepier, till, as he reached the foot of the tree, he could hardly move. Suddenly, out of the corner of his eye, Don Diego saw something falling from the tree, but he was too sleepyheaded to get out of the way. Then he felt something splashing over the top of his head, and Don Diego turned into a limestone rock.

The bird gave one last contented cry and fell asleep.

When Don Diego didn't return with the bird, Don Pedro announced that it was his turn to try his luck and his courage. He went the same way as his elder brother, and he, too, was strong and brave and quick on his journey. But he, too, ignored the old man begging for water in the desert, and when he reached the tree where the Adarna bird had its nest, he, too, was nearly fast asleep, and he couldn't avoid the bird droppings, and then he, too, was turned into a limestone rock.

Now it was Juan's turned to try, and everyone begged him not to go because he was lazy and stupid and good for nothing but sitting at home and entertaining his younger cousins with foolish tales. But he was determined to try. So Juan set out in the direction his brothers had gone. After many months he came to the desert and started across. It wasn't long before he met the old beggar, stooped and filthy and covered in stinking rags. Juan offered the beggar a sip of his water, and when the old man touched the jar to his lips he rose up into a splendid figure with a shining white beard. "Because you have been kind to me when others were cruel, I will give you a reward," said the old man.

"Oh, you don't have to," said Juan.

"That's exactly why I want to," said the old man. He handed Juan a lemon, a knife, and a bottle of holy water. "When you come to the tree of the enchanted Adarna bird, its song and its changing colors will make you want to sleep. But you must stay awake till it has finished its song. Cut your hand with this knife and squeeze lemon juice into your wound. The pain will keep you awake. When the bird finishes singing it will fall asleep and you can climb the tree and capture it with ease. Then you must sprinkle this water on the stones at the base of the tree. Oh, and one more thing: Watch out for bird droppings."

And the old man vanished.

Juan went on through the desert till he reached the limestone mountain. He climbed the mountain and as he reached the top, he heard the song of the Adarna bird. The song immediately made him sleepy, but he took out the knife and sliced his hand. Then he cut the lemon and squeezed the juice into his wound. As he approached the tree he kept squeezing the lemon in his palm, and so he was able to get to the foot of the tree with his eyes wide open.

Just as Juan was about to climb the tree, he saw out of the corner of his eye something falling from the branches. He leaped aside just as a huge multicolored mess fell on the rocks at his feet. Then the enchanted Adarna bird gave one more satisfied cry and stopped singing. It was fast asleep. Its feathers were a gentle, luminous, unchanging black.

Juan climbed easily up the tree and covered the bird with a cloth and put it in his shoulder bag. It never stirred. Then he climbed back down and sprinkled holy water on the stones at the foot of the tree. Up sprang a multitude of brave and handsome young men, among whom were Juan's two brothers. They brought the Adarna bird back to their father's kingdom, and the song of the bird immediately cured their father of his illness. As for Juan, he became king and ruled that country wisely and with an open heart. And as long as the Adarna bird sang, there was good health and prosperity among the people.

—Philippines (Roosevelt)

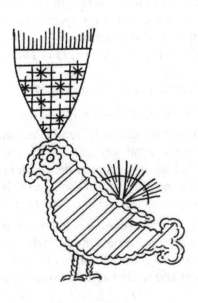

The Wise Rabbit and the Forest Sprite

Once upon a time there was a husband and his beautiful young wife. They lived alone and happily in the middle of the forest.

One day as they were eating lunch some soldiers came from the capitol with an order from the king. It said that the husband would have to go with the soldiers to fight a war in a distant land. Both the husband and the wife were shocked and grief-stricken. She barely had time to pack him some clothing and a few of his favorite foods. The soldiers were waiting for him. He called out to her, "I will come back to you," as they led him away into the forest.

Not far from their house, the man passed a certain tree where a spirit lived. The spirit looked out of the tree and saw the husband with his face twisted into a mask of grief. "What's the matter with this man?" the spirit asked itself. "Why is he so sad?"

So the spirit went to the man's house. It saw the man's wife standing at the door, staring after her husband. The spirit fell in love with the beautiful young wife. It changed itself into the shape of the husband and came walking back down the path out of the forest.

The wife had no idea that this was a spirit in her husband's form. She was just happy to see him and touch him again. So they lived together happily for a whole month.

Then the real husband came home on leave, only to find his wife working contentedly in her garden while someone who looked just like himself was lounging on the front porch smoking his favorite pipe.

"Who are you?" asked his wife in fear.

"I'm your husband," he replied. "Don't you know me?"

"How could you be my husband," she cried, "when my husband is sitting right there?"

He turned to the spirit-imposter and shouted, "Who are you, and what are you doing with my wife?"

"I'm her husband," the spirit replied. "Who do you think you are?"

The real husband was furious, and the wife was afraid that they might kill each other. "I'll live with both of you," she cried. "Just don't fight." But the real husband stared at the two of them, choked back a sob, and ran off into the forest.

Deep in the woods he sat down on a stone to weep. After a while he raised his head and noticed a rabbit sitting up on its hind legs across the path and staring at him in a frank, friendly manner.

"What's the matter?" asked the rabbit.

A look crossed the husband's face as if he were certainly going insane. "Don't be afraid," the rabbit said. "You look like a pretty nice guy, and maybe we can help each other."

"Help each other," said the husband. "How can you help me—you're a rabbit."

The rabbit said, "Believe me, I may be a rabbit, but I notice things. Like this tree spirit that's living with your wife, for instance. I know some things about him that maybe you don't."

This got the husband's attention. "What do you know about him?"

"The most important thing—like, how to get rid of him."

"How?"

"I'll show you—if you'll promise me a carrot a day from your garden and keep your dogs tied up."

"It's a promise."

So the husband took the rabbit with him to his house. The wife and the spirit husband came out to meet them. The rabbit sat down on the porch and asked the spirit, "Are you this woman's husband?"

The spirit quickly said, "Yes." Then the rabbit turned to the real husband, asked the same question, and got the same answer.

"We've got a problem here," said the rabbit, "but I know just how to solve it. Bring me a bottle with a good cork stopper." They brought him a bottle from the house. "Whoever can put himself into this bottle will get the wife."

"I can do that," said the spirit, and quick as a flash he was inside the bottle. The rabbit stuck in the cork, sealed it with wax, and threw it away in the deepest part of the forest.

The real husband and wife were as happy as they could be to be united again. They always made sure to leave a carrot for the wise rabbit every day and to keep their dogs tied up. And they lived happily ever after.

—Cambodia (Roosevelt)

Why Cat and Tiger Are No Longer Friends

A long time ago, when there were not too many human beings, all the animals knew how to talk. At that time, Cat and Tiger were still good friends. Cat was very nimble and skilled at catching other creatures to eat. But Tiger was clumsy and boisterous, and his efforts at hunting usually ended in failure.

One day, Tiger went to Cat's house and asked him, "Friend, will you teach me how to hunt as quietly and cleverly as you do?"

Cat said, "Friend, I will gladly help however I can. For, not to be critical, but I can see some ways that you could improve your technique."

So Cat went to work teaching Tiger how to hunt. At first the lessons went slowly. Tiger was large, slow, and stupid, and he kept tripping over his own big feet. But Cat patiently taught him all the tricks he used to slip stealthily up on his prey, and soon Tiger began to improve. As Cat saw that Tiger was becoming a better and better hunter, he thought to himself, "There are one or two tricks I'd better not teach him—I might need them later on."

Well, there came a time when Tiger thought he had learned everything Cat had to teach. Tiger had become quite a clever hunter, and he usually could count on catching plenty of game with all of his new tricks. But one day, he had been hunting all morning and caught nothing at all. His stomach was growling so that you could hear it in the treetops. He began to wonder if Cat had really taught him all of his tricks. Tiger's mind was so twisted with hunger that he thought, "Perhaps I'll just go over to Cat's house and try him out. It would make a good final exam."

So Tiger snuck up as stealthily as he could on Cat's little house. Cat was out in the yard chopping firewood and didn't seem to hear a thing. With a great effort of will Tiger quieted his stomach and crept out of the woods till he could almost touch the tip of Cat's tail. But at the last moment, as he was getting set to pounce, his big foot snapped a twig. In a flash, Cat leaped onto the trunk of a nearby tree and scrambled to the top.

Tiger pounced, but he came up empty. There he stood at the foot of the tree, trying hard to smile. "Friend," he said, "I never knew you could climb trees that way. Why didn't you teach me that trick?"

"First," Cat hissed, "I don't see any friends here—just an ungrateful wretch who wants to have me for lunch. Second, I always had a feeling it might come to this. A wise teacher stays one step ahead of his pupil. Now go away. Our lessons are over."

Since that time, Cat and Tiger have never been friends. Tiger has been hunting on his own and doing pretty well. But there are still a few things he wishes he had learned from Cat.

—Vietnam (Roosevelt)

Brotherhood

Once upon a time there were two brothers who lived in a village. Their parents had passed away when they were small. The two brothers shared a little house, farming and hunting for their food. They were everything to each other.

One day, the older brother fell in love with a girl in the village, and they were engaged to be married. The older brother, by custom, went to live with his wife's family, and he left his brother behind, alone.

They both grew wheat, now in separate fields. At the end of summer, the wheat was ripe for harvest. Both brothers went to the fields the night before the harvest to sleep in the fields and protect them from animals and thieves.

At midnight the older brother thought, "How is my brother? How is he getting along without me? Will he have enough food for the winter?" He decided to bring some of his wheat to his brother, without telling his wife. So he cut a bunch of wheat and started off to his younger brother's field.

Meanwhile, at the other field, the younger brother was thinking of his brother too. "How is my brother doing?" he thought. "Is he able to take good care of his wife? I've heard that they're going to have a baby—will they have enough wheat to last them through the winter?" He decided to give his older brother some of his wheat. So he cut a bunch from his field and carried it off toward his brother's field.

Halfway between their fields they met. In the moonlight they recognized each other, and each one understood right away what the other was thinking and feeling and doing. They dropped their bundles of wheat, hugged each other, and wept.

—Vietnam (Roosevelt)

Areca Nut, Betel Plant, and Limestone

A long time ago there was a family with two sons, Sang and Thanh. These two looked so much alike that no one could distinguish which was the older and which was the younger.

When the brothers were grown to manhood, a teacher in their village by the name of Tran invited them both to his house for dinner. He brought out one bowl of rice and a single pair of chopsticks and called Sang and Thanh to the table. Sang passed the bowl to his brother to eat first. In that way, Tran knew that Sang was the older brother. So he gave Sang his daughter to marry.

Sang and his wife made a beautiful couple. But after they were married, Sang and Thanh were not as close as they had been before. This made Thanh so unhappy that he left his home and wandered off into the forest with no destination in mind. He came to a river, and there he stopped, waiting for a boat to take him across. But no boat came.

Thanh was so sad that he just sat by the river, weeping. In that place he died and was transformed into an areca nut tree.

When Sang found out that his brother had left home, he immediately went out to look for him. He asked many people, but no one knew where Thanh had gone. Finally, he reached the river where his brother had died. When he found some articles of Thanh's clothing there by the areca nut tree, he realized that his brother was dead. In his grief, Sang began hitting his head against the trunk of the tree and died on the spot. When he died, he was transformed into a limestone rock.

At home, Sang's wife was so worried about her husband and brother-in-law that she went out searching for them. When she reached the riverbank, she knew that Sang and Thanh had both died there. She threw herself down on the limestone rock and cried and cried until she cried and starved herself to death. And then she was transformed into a betel plant, still clinging tightly around the limestone rock.

Some years later, a king was passing along the riverbank when he saw the areca nut tree, the limestone rock, and the betel plant together there. He had heard the story of Thanh, Sang, and his wife, and it filled him with emotion. He took a few leaves from the betel plant and a piece of areca nut and put them in his mouth to try them, and he found that they tasted good. When he spit out the juice on the limestone rock, he was surprised to see it turn a beautiful deep red color. The king thought that the color symbolized the deep love between the husband, brother, and wife. He ordered his people to build an altar there to the three of them. From that time on, many people in Vietnam know to chew betel leaves and areca nut to make their lips red. At weddings, it is still the custom to bring betel leaves and areca nut as gifts for the bridegroom's family. It is also used as snacks by the wedding guests, which is why the Vietnamese people often say, "Betel leaves are the start of conversation."

—Vietnam (Roosevelt)

The Bunch of Chopsticks

Once there was a father who had three sons. But the sons were always fighting one another, and the father was sad. One day at dinnertime the sons didn't come to the table because they were fighting, as usual. The father called his sons and asked his eldest son to bring him a bunch of chopsticks.

The father took the bunch of chopsticks and tied them together with a ribbon. He passed it around to his sons and asked them each to try and break it. No one could break the bunch of chopsticks.

Then the father took three chopsticks out of the bunch and gave one to each of his sons. "Try and break it now," he told them. Each son easily broke the single chopstick.

The father smiled and said, "All of you are like these chopsticks. If you are united, no one can harm you. But if you are always fighting, then anyone can come between you and do you evil—and you will even do evil to yourselves."

The sons understood what their father was trying to teach them. From then on they did their best to express only loving and caring for each other.

—Vietnam (Roosevelt)

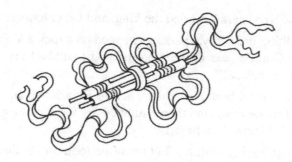

The Ghost Pig

This story happened to my family.

I used to live in a really small village, only five houses, on the edge of the rain forest. One night it was raining hard, and I couldn't sleep. I heard a sound of an animal in the yard behind the house, so I opened the window and looked around. I saw a pig using its nose to dig up the ground next to the lemon tree.

I called my grandfather, because I wanted him to kill that pig. My grandfather woke up, got his gun, and looked out the window. He saw that pig digging at the ground. He looked at that pig for a really long time. Then he shook his head and told me to shut the window and go back to sleep.

The next morning I opened the window and looked out by the lemon tree where the pig had been the night before. But I couldn't see anything. The ground was undisturbed, as if nothing had been touched.

I went to my grandmother and asked her why? Her face looked so sad for a moment, and then she told me.

"Three years ago we had a female pig here at home, and that pig got pregnant and had one little piglet. But because the mother was sick for some days before giving birth, both the mother and the son died.

"We buried those pigs, mother and son, in separate places, the mother in the forest, the piglet by the lemon tree, where you saw the mother pig digging last night.

"This is the third time we have seen the mother pig's spirit come back, digging to find her son."

Do you believe me? I guarantee, this is a true story.

—Vietnam (Roosevelt)

Gopal the Jester

Once there was a king in India named Raja Krishna who had a court jester named Gopal. People thought that Gopal was a fool, but in his foolishness there was wisdom. Gopal could say the most outrageous things to the king, things that would get anyone else jailed or killed, and the way he would say them would only make the king laugh.

One morning Gopal was on his way to town when he met the king and his royal entourage. The king said, "Good morning, Gopal. Where are you going alone and on foot?"

"To Tampal," Gopal replied. "And where are you going, your highness, in your carriage with all these lackeys?"

"We are going to the royal park," replied the king, and the entourage moved on.

As the king was walking in the royal park, he stepped on a rock and stubbed his toe. In a royal rage, he shouted, "I saw Gopal's face in the morning and I stubbed my toe. He brought me bad luck! Bring him to me at the palace!"

The soldiers brought Gopal bound in chains before Raja Krishna. The king said, "Gopal, I saw your miserable face this morning and then I stubbed my toe. You brought me bad luck." Turning to his soldiers, he said, "Throw him in jail."

Gopal stood very still, saying nothing. But from the look on his face, the king knew he had something to say.

"Alright, Gopal," said the king, "tell me what you're thinking."

"Excuse me, your highness," said Gopal. "You saw my miserable face this morning and you stubbed your toe. But I saw your face this morning and I'm going to jail. So tell me, who brought who bad luck?"

The king couldn't help himself—he burst out laughing. Then he ordered Gopal to be released from his chains, and he gave him a bag of gold for his foolish wit.

—India, Gujerati (Roosevelt)

The Lamp on the Tower

Birbal was a servant at the court of King Akbar. One day for his entertainment, the king put out word that anyone who could spend the night submerged to his chest in the moat in front of the palace would win his weight in gold. Many poor men tried, but none could endure the cold for the entire night.

Then Birbal tried. When dawn cast its first light over the moat, he was still submerged to his chest, staring fixedly at the tower of the palace.

He was wrapped in warm robes and taken before the king. "How did you do it?" the king demanded to know. "What was your secret?"

"Your Highness," said Birbal, "I merely stared at the light of the lamp at the top of your palace tower, and the sight gave me courage to endure."

"You have cheated then," declared Akbar, "You used the fire of the lamp to warm you. For that you have forfeited your prize."

Birbal tried to protest but it was no use. He was dragged from the hall and tossed out without further ceremony.

The next day, there was Birbal, sitting in front of the moat with a pot of rice before him—but no fire. He sat there for three days.

At the end of the third day he was brought before the King. "I must know," the king demanded. "What are you trying to do sitting in front of the palace with a pot of rice but no fire for the past three days?"

"Your Highness, I am cooking the rice."

"But you have no fire!"

"I am using the flame from the lamp at the top of the palace tower."

"Fool, that is nowhere near enough to cook the rice."

"Ah, King, if it was near enough to keep me warm while I stood all night in the cold waters of the moat, it must be warm enough to cook a pot of rice. So I will wait there until the rice is cooked—or until I receive my prize."

The king had to admit that he had been bested, not once, but twice, and Birbal received two times his weight in gold.

—India, Gujerati (Senn)

The Hand of God

Once there was a king whose *wazier,* his chief advisor, was an optimist. Whatever happened in the kingdom, no matter how apparently unfortunate, the *wazier* would say, "Surely something good will come from this. This is the hand of God."

Sometimes the king just didn't care to hear this.

One day the king and his *wazier* went into the jungle to hunt. There they met a band of soldiers from an enemy kingdom. There was an exchange of fire, and before the hostile band could be driven off, one of their arrows shattered the king's thumb.

"Oh, dear," clucked the *wazier.* "But surely some good will come of this. This is the hand of God."

This was a moment when the king did not want to hear this at all. "The hand of God, you say! But what about my hand! Have you no respect!" And he ordered his wazier thrown into jail.

When the *wazier's* friends came to visit him in jail, they said, "What a terrible thing that this has happened to you!" But the *wazier* just said, "Surely some good will come of this. It's the hand of God."

The next week, the king went hunting again. This time he went to the border of another hostile kingdom, and again he ran into a raiding party. This time his company was entirely overrun. The captain of the raiding party went from prisoner to prisoner, inspecting them for physical imperfections. Those who were healthy and unblemished he brought back to his kingdom to sell as slaves. Those who were wounded or lame he released. And because of his shattered thumb, the king was released.

When the king got back to his palace he immediately sent for his *wazier* from jail. And when he saw his old advisor he clasped him in his arms and lamented, "My old friend, your wisdom has come back to haunt me. If it had not been for my shattered thumb I would have been sold into slavery today. Can you ever forgive me for putting you in jail for no cause but my own vanity?"

"But certainly, my king, for surely some good did come of it. If I had not been in jail I would have been hunting with you, and I would have been sold into slavery myself."

And together the king and his *wazier* intoned, "It was the hand of God!"

—India, Gujerati (Senn)

The Dutti Malen

Once upon a time there was a father, a mother, and two children. The family was of the class of people called Bharwad—people who live only for today with no thought of tomorrow.

There came a time when the family's well was running dry. They began to worry that they wouldn't have water for today, let alone for tomorrow. So they went to the local sadhu, a holy man or priest, to ask him what they should do.

"Cut the fingers of your son and your daughter," he told them, "and drip the blood into the well. That will bring the water back."

The daughter overheard her father and mother discussing the sadhu's advice. She was very scared. She thought her parents were going to kill them. So she went to her brother and told him, "We've got to run away. Tomorrow when mother is braiding my hair, you come and ask for something to eat. Then, when mother goes to make the food, we'll run away."

And that's what they did. The next morning as the mother was braiding the daughter's hair, the son came in and asked for food. When the mother went to prepare it, the children ran away to the forest.

They ran till they came to the orchard of a Dutti Malen—a gossip—who grew fruit to take to market. The orchard was fallow, but when the two children entered in, it suddenly burst into leaf and fruit. Neighbors who saw it happen ran to tell the Dutti Malen. Meanwhile, the two children ate and ate from the orchard till they got tired of eating fruit. They decided that the boy would walk to town and trade or beg for some cooked food.

As the boy came into the town, the king and queen just happened to be riding in their carriage to look on their people. When they saw the boy walking along the road, the queen, who was childless, said, "Look at that handsome boy. He looks like an orphan or a runaway. Let's take him in and raise him as our own."

The king agreed. So they picked up the boy and took him to their palace. The boy was so dazzled by the luxury of his new surroundings that he forgot all about his sister, waiting for him back in the Dutti Malen's orchard.

Meanwhile, the Dutti Malen came out to her orchard to see what all the fuss was about. She saw her orchard miraculously burst into leaf and fruit, and then she saw the girl, sitting forlornly under one of the trees. "Ah," the Dutti Malen thought, "this girl is the cause of my good fortune. I will adopt her and raise her as my own." So while the boy was adopted by the king and queen, the girl was adopted by the Dutti Malen.

Several years went by.

One day the girl was drawing water at a community well when her brother, the king's adopted son, stopped to water his horse, and there he saw his sister. He didn't recognize her, but he thought only that she was the most beautiful girl he had ever set eyes on. To get her attention, he tossed a pebble at her feet.

She looked up at him on his horse and knew right away who he was. But because it was forbidden for a poor young girl to directly address a prince, she began to sing a song.

> "Brother, why do you throw a stone at me?
> Don't you remember how we left our home
> Because our parents meant to shed our blood?
> Don't you remember how we ate the fruit
> In the Dutti Malen's orchard?
> And how you left me to go to town for food,
> And how I never saw you again?"

The Prince heard her singing, but he didn't realize her song was about him. He only knew that he had fallen desperately in love with her. He went to his parents, the king and queen, and told them that he had found the girl he wished to marry. But when he told them who it was, they said that it was impossible. She was much too poor and had no position at all—the adopted daughter of a Dutti Malen.

The prince took to his bed and would not eat, drink, or speak. His parents feared for his life. So finally they sent an ambassador to the home of the Dutti Malen. "The king and queen have ordered your daughter to present herself before the court."

The Dutti Malen was terrified that her daughter had committed some crime. She didn't understand that these were the formalities that preceded an offer of marriage. When her friends and neighbors finally explained it to her, she was as overjoyed as she had been fearful. "This girl I adopted is once again the cause of my good fortune," she exclaimed.

But when she told the girl that she was to be presented to the court for marriage to the prince, the girl only put her hands over her face and sang through her tears:

> "Brother, why do you throw a stone at me?
> Don't you remember how we left our home
> Because our parents meant to shed our blood?
> Don't you remember how we ate the fruit
> In the Dutti Malen's orchard?
> And how you left me to go to town for food,
> And how I never saw you again?"

While they painted her hands with henna, she wept and sang:

> "Brother, why do you throw a stone at me?
> Don't you remember how we left our home
> Because our parents meant to shed our blood?
> Don't you remember how we ate the fruit
> In the Dutti Malen's orchard?
> And how you left me to go to town for food,
> And how I never saw you again?"

On her way to the mosque she sang the same sad song. Under the wedding tent with her husband as the contract was being signed by the king and the Dutti Malen, she sang the song, but no one noticed. On the wedding night in the canopied bed with her brother/husband, she sang the song again:

> "Brother, why do you throw a stone at me?
> Don't you remember how we left our home
> Because our parents meant to shed our blood?
> Don't you remember how we ate the fruit
> In the Dutti Malen's orchard?
> And how you left me to go to town for food,
> And how I never saw you again?"

And now her brother remembered who she was, and why she had always seemed so familiar to him. But now they were married, and it was an abomination before the gods. "Why didn't you tell me before?" he cried.

"I told you every time I saw you, every chance I had," she wept. In disgrace, he took his dagger and stabbed it into his heart. And when the flames of his funeral pyre were leaping high, she jumped into it and was consumed with him. And so they were together after all.

—India, Gujerati (Senn)

The Surprised Thief

Here is a Gujerati (Hindu) version of a story that is told in Muslim communities about Nasrudin.

One night a thief snuck into a garden and filled the pockets of his coat with fruits. Suddenly the owner of the garden came out of the house and caught the thief red-handed. "What are you doing in my garden?" he demanded.

"Sir," said the thief, "I didn't come here of my own desire—a strong wind picked me up and blew me over your wall and dropped me here."

The owner said, "But why did you pick my fruits?"

"Sir, I never picked those fruits—the same storm shook the branches and dropped down those fruits."

The owner stared at the thief. "Then what," he said, "are the fruits doing in the pockets of your coat?"

The thief put his hands to his pockets and stared back. "Believe me when I tell you, sir," he said, "that it really surprises me, too."

—India, Gujerati (Roosevelt)

The Monkey's Heart

Long long ago there was a monkey named Kisku. He lived in a tree, the fruit of which tasted like honey. The tree stood on the banks of a river, and in that river lived a crocodile named Raju. Kisku and Raju were friends. Many days they would spend together, Kisku in the tree eating sweet fruit, Raju sunning himself on the bank, the two of them conversing philosophically.

The crocodile told his wife about his pleasant afternoons with Kisku. But when she thought of the monkey in that tree eating fruit all day, it made her hungry. "I bet that monkey's heart tastes sweeter than honey," she said. "If you love me, you'll bring me that monkey's heart to eat."

Raju was horrified. "How could I sacrifice my friend just to bring you his heart to eat!" But Raju's wife wept big crocodile tears and threatened to leave him for someone who knew how to treat a lady. In the end, Raju gave in and promised to bring her the monkey's heart.

So Raju went to the riverbank and called to Kisku. "Come on down. My wife is inviting you for dinner." The monkey was very excited. He had never been invited to another creature's home for dinner before. So he came down and got on Raju's back, and they swam off toward his crocodile home.

As they swam, Raju called to Kisku, "Isn't it true, my friend, that there is good and bad to be found in every experience?"

"Yes indeed, my old companion, I'm sure that this is true."

"This afternoon, for example, I am giving you an experience such as you have never had in your entire life."

"This is very true, my friend, and I am grateful."

"You are crossing the river on a crocodile's back, on your way to visit a crocodile's home."

"And a great pleasure and a privilege it is, I am most aware," offered Kisku.

"Of course, there is one feature that might perhaps be considered, if not strictly a negative, at least a hindrance to your complete enjoyment," said the crocodile.

"I assure you that I will understand if your domestic arrangements are not all that I am accustomed to," said Kisku.

"Ah, yes," said Raju, "that would be most gracious, and, I would add, most wise, given the situation with my wife."

"Ah, your wife. And how is that most beautiful and accomplished lady, your wife?"

"She is as she is," replied Raju, "She's my life partner and a woman of incomparable appetite. In fact, when we were discussing this evening's meal, she made what you or I might consider a most unusual request."

"And what was that request, my friend?"

"My wife has got it into her head that she would like to dine on a monkey's heart. Watch for that low-hanging branch, my dear."

"And what did you tell your wife about this strange compulsion?"

"I told her that it would be a terrible thing for me to do to a cherished companion." They were approaching the door to the crocodile's house.

"I am most relieved," said Kisku. "Of course your wife agreed with you and renounced her evil desire."

"On the contrary," said Raju, "she threatened me with divorce. Welcome to my house, friend."

"Beloved Raju, noblest of reptiles," the monkey said in his most honeyed tones. "It would give me great honor if I could gratify your wife's craving and provide her with a sweet monkey's heart. But alas, I have left my own heart at the top of the tree where I live. I never take it with me on long journeys, lest I lose it to an enemy. But if you take me back there right away, I will gladly fetch it down and give it to you and your wife, as a token of my friendship and regard."

The crocodile was touched by Kisku's offer and also relieved that he wouldn't have to kill his friend to get his heart. So he turned around and rushed back to the other shore, right up to the base of the monkey's tree. Kisku leaped from Raju's back and scampered into the topmost branches. "O crocodile you spiny fool," he cried. "When have you heard of any creature keeping his heart apart from himself? You have been blinded by your own evil designs. Never again will we converse without at least the length of a tree trunk between us."

Crocodile slunk back into the water, ashamed, and had to endure the reproaches of his wife as well as the taunts of his former friend.

—India, Malayalam (Roosevelt)

The Good-hearted Daughter

Once upon a time there was a man named Ravi who had a good-hearted daughter named Mina. Mina's mother died when she was young, and Ravi married again. His new wife had a daughter of her own and they were friendly to Mina for a while, but then they turned cruel and made her do all the work around the house.

One day, Mina's stepsister ordered her to weave some cotton cloth to make her a dress. As Mina was weaving, the cotton thread suddenly formed itself into the shape of a man's head and flew off into the jungle. Mina jumped up and ran after it. She followed the head till it came to a clearing where there was a little hut. The head went inside, and Mina followed it. In the corner of the hut was an old woman lying on a cot, sick. She was unable to help herself, so Mina went to fetch her warm water and milk.

The old woman was grateful to Mina for her help. She told Mina that as her reward she should take a wooden box from the other corner, bring it home, and open it there. Mina took a box from the corner, brought it to her house, and opened it. Out stepped a tall, quiet lad who seemed to Mina the handsomest fellow in the world. They were married, and Mina went to live with him in a palace.

When Mina's stepmother heard how Mina had found a husband, she wanted her daughter to try it too. Mina's stepsister sat weaving at the loom until the thread rose up in the shape of a man's head and flew away. She chased the head through the jungle till she came to the hut in the clearing. She went into the hut, but when she saw the sick old woman she didn't try to help. She only asked her, "Where is my box?"

The old woman pointed to some boxes in the corner, and the stepsister grabbed the biggest one she could carry. When she got it home and opened it, out stepped a little old man, evil-tempered, humpbacked, and leaning on a stick. "You belong to me," he said, and he married her. The old man took her to live in a filthy, desolate hovel, and there she worked her fingers to the bone.

—India, Urdu (Roosevelt)

The Strongest of All Creatures

Once there was a pair of mice who had a beautiful daughter. They wanted her to get married, and as she was so very beautiful, they wanted the strongest and handsomest creature they could find to be her husband. So the father mouse set out in search for a proper bridegroom for his daughter.

On his way, he saw the sun, and he called up to him, "Oh Sun, you are surely the strongest of all creatures. No one can hide from you. Will you marry my beautiful daughter?"

The sun replied, "I'm not the strongest of all—the cloud can cover me and hide my face."

So the mouse went to the cloud and said, "Oh Cloud, the sun says you are the strongest of all creatures. Will you marry my beautiful daughter?"

Cloud said, "I'm not the strongest of all—the wind can blow me all over the earth."

So the mouse went to the wind and said, "Oh Wind, Cloud says you are the strongest of all creatures. Will you marry my beautiful daughter?"

Wind said, "I'm not the strongest of all—the wall can stop me dead in my tracks."

So the mouse went to the wall and said, "Oh Wall, the wind says you are the strongest of all creatures. Will you marry my beautiful daughter?"

The wall said, "I'm not the strongest of all. There's a mouse living underneath me chewing holes in me day and night."

So the father mouse went to the mouse who lived in the wall and asked him, "Oh Mouse, strongest and handsomest creature of all, would you marry my beautiful daughter?"

The mouse drew himself up to his full height and dignity and answered, "Sure!"

So the two mice got married and lived happily ever after, and their children were beautiful, plentiful, and strong enough to chew down a wall.

—India, Urdu (Roosevelt)

Planting Gold

Once upon a time Nasruddin was digging holes on the side of the road and putting grains of gold in those holes. Eventually the king passed by and asked him what on earth he thought he was doing?

He said, "I'm planting gold. I'll water it and I'll get some more of it."

The King found it interesting. "He might just be on to something," he thought. He asked Nasruddin if he wanted to go into business together. "You could take the gold from my palace and farm it on shares—we'll each take half the crop when it comes up."

Nasruddin took all the gold from the palace and handed it out to the poor and needy.

After a week he went back to the palace to report to the king.

"I have bad news, partner," he said. "It didn't rain for the whole week, and our crops are completely wiped out."

The king said, "That's ridiculous. How could all that gold be wiped out just by a little drought?"

"Ah," Nasruddin replied serenely. "It must be by the very same set of laws that would have made it grow when I planted it in the ground."

And Nasruddin left the palace untouched by the king's wrath. But the story teaches us what greed can do to our thinking.

—Pakistan, Urdu (Mather)

The Milkman and the Monkeys

Once upon a time there was a greedy milkman. He liked to add water to his milk so that he would have larger quantities to sell and he could make more money. Customers were complaining about the quality of the milk he was selling. But he didn't care because he was the only milkman in the area, and he was doing just fine.

One day he decided to start selling coconuts. He filled a cart full of the shaggy pods and he started on the way from the village to the city. After a while he felt sleepy. He thought he would stop in the shade of a grove of trees and rest for couple of hours, and then go on his way.

He was awakened by the sound of a coconut falling right next to his head. His cart was empty. There was a tribe of monkeys in the trees above his head, and they had stolen all of his coconuts. They were throwing them, one at him and one into the river.

The milkman yelled at them, "What do you think you're doing?"

"You cheated the people when you added water to their milk," the monkeys chattered. "So we're learning how to play your game. One coconuts goes to you and one goes in the river." And the monkeys went on tossing the coconuts, one at him and one into the river—all the while yelling "MILK! WATER! MILK! WATER!"—until half of the milkman's coconuts had floated away.

The milkman never watered his milk from that day forward. But between milk and coconuts, he did pretty well anyhow.

—Pakistan, Urdu (Mather)

The Sparrow and His Friends

Once upon a time a hunter went into the jungle to hunt for wild birds. He spread his net across a clearing, and after a few minutes, a sparrow flew into it and was trapped.

The sparrow pleaded with the hunter for his freedom. "I'm so small," he cried, "that if you sell me you won't get any money at all, and if you eat me there won't be enough flesh on my bones to satisfy you."

"Such an intelligent bird," said the hunter. "I won't sell you, nor will I eat you. I'll keep you in a cage by my bedside and listen to your good advice." So he carried the sparrow home and shut it in a cage. All night the sparrow hung its head and was silent.

The next morning, when the hunter was getting ready to go to the jungle, he asked the sparrow, "Do you have any message you would like me to take to your friends?"

"Tell them that I am shut up in a cage and sick with loneliness and anxiety."

The hunter went to the jungle and spread his net. Then he called out to the birds in the trees, "Your friend the sparrow whom I captured yesterday wants you to know that he is shut up in a cage and feeling very lonely without your company."

At his words, one of the other sparrows gave a sharp cry, toppled from his branch, and fell like a stone to the ground. "My God," said the hunter, "the message has killed him!" He folded his net and rushed home to tell the caged sparrow. But when he did, the sparrow gave a cry, toppled off his perch, and fell with a thump to the floor of the cage.

"No, not again!" cried the hunter, and he opened the cage, picked up the bird, and carried it sadly to the open window. But when he tossed it out the window, the sparrow spread its wings, and flew straight to the top of a nearby tree.

"I knew my friends would know what I should do to gain my freedom!" he chirped.

And then he sang to the hunter:

"If something comes into your hand,
Hold it tight, enjoy the getting,
But if you lose it, let it go—
Don't waste time regretting."

—Pakistan, Urdu (Roosevelt)

The Honest Woodsman

Once upon a time, there was a poor woodsman who had a wife and five children to feed. One day as the poor man was chopping wood by the riverside, his only good axe suddenly slipped out of his grasp and fell into the water. The poor man put his head in his hands and wept loudly. His only source of income to earn money was gone in the river.

As he sat there weeping and crying for his axe, he suddenly saw a dazzling light rising out of the depths of the river. The simple man stopped crying and began to get scared. He was trying to figure out what this bright light could possibly be. Just then a head and a torso rose out of the river, a very big man with enormous wings.

The poor man thought, "It's either an angel or a *djinn*."

Angel or *djinn*, the creature held up an axe with a golden head that shone like the sun. "Is this yours?" the creature asked him.

The poor man was very happy for a moment, but then he looked more closely at the golden axe. "No," he said, "that it's not my axe. Mine was made of steel, and this one is made of gold."

The angel went back into the water and a moment later came up with a silver axe that shone like the moon. "Is this yours?" it asked him.

The poor man said, "I'm sorry, but no, mine is steel and this one is silver."

Once again the angel went back into the river and brought up an old, beat-up steel axe. "That's it! That's my axe!" the honest old woodsman cried, and he was as happy as he could be. "Now I can work and have something to sell and feed my family!"

"Go home," the angel said. "Today you won't have to work to get food for your family. Just go home and see what you find there waiting for you."

So the poor man went straight home, and as he came into his house, he found the table covered with fresh and delicious foods. He told his wife the whole story about the angel. "I know something about it," she said, and she took him to the shed and showed him the gold and silver axes. She told him, "The angel came and gave us these axes and these rich foods. He said, 'Your husband is a very honest man, and that's why I am giving you these axes to give to him.'"

The poor man went to the big city and sold the golden and silver axes for a great deal of money. Then he bought a new house, started a brand-new business, and did very well. After a while, he started collecting old axes, just for a hobby. In time, many years after the old man's death, his children sold that axe collection for lots and lots of money.

And that's why they say: An honest man is worth more than silver and gold.

—Pakistan, Urdu (Mather)

Patience

Once there was a king with seven daughters, each more beautiful than the next. The king was a wise and generous ruler who was always being invited to neighboring countries for visits. One day the king was getting ready to travel to a foreign land, and before he left he asked each of his daughters what she would like him to bring her back as a gift. The first six daughters made their requests, but the seventh was deep in her morning prayers when the king came to ask her. All she would say, as Allah requires, was, "Patience, Father, patience."

"What is this Patience she asks me to bring her?" the king thought, completely puzzled by this strange request. But the caravan was leaving, and he could not wait for explanations.

He completed his embassy visit and had ample time to shop for his first six daughters' gifts. But when it came to finding something for the youngest, he was at a loss. "Where do I find Patience?" he asked at every shop, but no one had any idea.

Finally he looked into a mysterious little shop in an out-of-the-way corner of the bazaar. There were many antique manuscripts and curious looking relics on the walls, and an old, old shopkeeper with a piercing gaze from beneath craggy brows. He looked expectantly at the king as if he knew the king's purpose better than the king himself.

"I'm looking for something for my youngest daughter," he began hesitantly. "She asked for Patience, but no one can tell me where to find it."

The old shopkeeper broke right in. "Yes, yes, yes," he said, "I've got just the thing." And he reached under the counter and brought out a cheap-looking tin cylinder. "In this container she will find Patience, and much, much more. I know the hearts of women and men, and I assure you, this is her very heart's desire."

The shopkeeper opened the cylinder and drew out a worn, inexpensive paper fan.

"It doesn't look very nice," said the king. "Are you certain she'll like it?"

"She won't just like it—she'll love it!" said the strange old merchant, and there was something in his voice that made the king believe. So he paid the price and took the fan home to his daughter.

All the gifts had been distributed to the six older sisters when the king came to his youngest, and sadly he held out the little tin cylinder. "You said you wanted Patience," he told her, "and I couldn't find it anywhere. So I brought you this instead."

"Oh, Father, I just meant that I couldn't talk because I was praying. So I expected nothing. You're sweet for even trying to find something for me. For that I'll treasure it always." And she graciously took the cylinder to her room. There she opened it and took out the old, brittle, paper fan.

She held it this way and that, regarding it in the fond light of a daughter's love. And suddenly it leaped out of her hand, and before her stood a handsome prince.

When the princess got over her surprise and heard his story, she insisted that he go to her father right away and repeat it, which he did.

"I was the son of the King of Iran," he told the king, "placed under a spell by an evil witch who wanted to marry me against my will. She turned me into that cheap paper fan, saying that now I would find out what it felt like to be scorned. I would never regain my own form, she said, until a princess would hold me in her hand and love me. But I thought no princess would ever love me in that humble form, so I resigned myself to living trapped inside that fan forever.

"That old magician of a shopkeeper bought me, knowing he was not the one to redeem me, but knowing that he could keep me safe and sound till the right one came along. And when you came in asking for Patience for your daughter, he knew right away that the moment was at hand, for hadn't I had time to learn patience, shut up for years in that dark tin can?"

"If this is your story, then you must be destined to marry my daughter," said the king.

"If she will have me," said the prince.

"I will," said the princess.

"Then it is the will of Allah," said the prince.

"Do you like your gift, my dear?" asked the King.

"I don't just like it," she said. "I LOVE IT!"

—Pakistan, Urdu (Mather)

The end crowns all.

—Urdu proverb

NOTES ON THE STORIES

Introduction

"The Education Tree."   A Pakistani wisdom tale about the importance of learning that I have not encountered elsewhere. The advantages for an ethnic group with cultural stories like this in encountering the challenges of a new educational system are evident.

Chapter 1

"Educated and Uneducated."   Another fable about the uses and limitations of book learning. Found in the *Panchatantra,* a 2,200-year-old Indian story collection.

Chapter 2

"Hot Pepper and Boiling Water."   Tortoise is the chief trickster hero of the Yoruba people of present-day Nigeria. There is a parallel version from Benin featuring Hare in Holt and Mooney's *More Ready-to-Tell Tales* (71). For more tales in this Nigerian Tortoise cycle, see notes 51–54 below.

Chapter 3

"The House Between Earth and Sky."   A classic wonder tale found all over Europe and the European colonies. The best-known North American version is in Chase's *The Jack Tales* (47, 191n).

Latin America

"Juan El Huevon."   Submitted by Loreto Martinez, from his grandmother. A tale from the popular series of "Lazy Juan" stories, known by various names (Jack, Jean, Hans, Juan, and so forth.) in any country where the Judeo-Christian name John is common. In England, Scotland, Ireland, and America, these tales are known as "Jack tales" (Chase, 1943). "Juan Bobo's Pig" from Puerto Rico (see note) and "Lazy Juan" from the Philippines are others in this same genre, but "Does Your Father Have Horns on his Head?" from Yemen is a close relative as well. "Juan El Huevon" gives an interesting twist to the hero's name.

"The Hen of the Quince Hills."   Submitted by Juan Muñoz, from his mother. A local legend, like so many Mexican folktales, that evokes the cultural and religious collisions of the Spanish conquest. The birds that can transform themselves into a giant snake is an image of the ancient Mayan god Quetzalcoatl, whose emblem is the feathered serpent.

"You Can't Please Everybody."   Submitted by Carlos Garcia, from his aunt and great-aunt. A well-known fable with versions from all over the world, including the earliest collections of Aesop. In some versions there is an additional incident in which the donkey falls from a bridge, with its inevitable concluding pun ("If you try to please everyone, you'll wind up losing your . . . ").

"The Water of Life."   Submitted by Pedro Martinez. A folktale with parallels in Grimm ("God-father Death") and many other collections. There is often an additional episode in which Death stands at the head or the foot of a patient's bed to indicate whether the patient will live or die. The doctor cures a king or king's daughter by reversing the bed, but he forfeits his own life. An excellent version crafted by Doug Lipman can be found in Holt and Mooney's *Ready-to-Tell Tales* (74).

"Three Pieces of Advice."   Submitted by Bandy Aguilar. A classic riddling folktale, combining the widely known motifs of a journey to find both fortune and wisdom with a poignant migratory situation so common in Mexican-American family life.

"El Sombreron."   Submitted by Letitia Vargas, from her mother. A local legend with an ancient central character (the Devil in his local guise) and a twist that could come from recent third-world industrial accidents—a wonderful example of folklore constantly updating itself.

"What the Dogs Saw."   Submitted by Marielena and Annabelle Medina, from Marielena's mother. A hair-raising local legend from the Mexican state of Guerrero that incorporates a range of folk beliefs about the supernatural. This story was told to me in tandem—Marielena, the mother, in Spanish and Annabelle, the daughter, in English—after my Parents' Night presentation early in the residency at Roosevelt. The moment when the central character discovers that the candle she thinks she is carrying is actually a bone provides a natural moment for a jump and scream from the storyteller—which, if correctly performed, should make the whole audience fly backwards in their chairs.

"The Black Cat Ate His Soul."   Submitted by Carlos Garcia, from his aunt and great-aunt. An example of the kind of behavior-modifying legend that parents find very useful. Many supernatural legends display this kind of didactic purpose.

"The Horseman in the Whirlwind."   Submitted by Maritza Tenorio. Another local legend that combines supernatural beliefs with lessons about proper feminine behavior.

"The Snake Husband."   Submitted by Maria Rojas, from her brother. A legend, like "The Hen of the Quince Hills," that carries the memory of ancient Mayan symbols, notably the magical serpent, which can be snake, bird, or human in turn. This story was told to me in the Senn cafeteria by a girl who was not otherwise part of the residency project.

"Buried Treasure."   Submitted by Carlos Garcia from his uncle, Rodrigo Baca from his grandfather ("Gold or Charcoal"), Juan Tello from memory ("Pesos"), and Jorge Virhuez from his grandmother ("The Blue Light"). Several legends of the search for gold that carry the traditional belief that buried gold can only be uncovered by one who is worthy, through secret wisdom or purity of heart—beliefs that come from the realm, not of literal treasure-hunting, but of traditional alchemy.

"La Llorona."   Submitted variously by Alma Perez, Carlos Garcia, Teresa Tello, Ivelise Rodriguez, Jairo Uribe, Sandra Villanueva, Raul Jimenez, and Rafael Sanchez. Quite simply the most widespread legend in the Latin world, still ardently believed and retold in countless variants. The recent Susan Smith variations show the continuing adaptive power of folklore, even as the La Malinche versions show the ability of folktales to embody an entire culture's core conflicts.

"The Fairy Falin."   Submitted by Keila Flores, from her mother. A Guatemalan variant of the "Kind and Wicked Step-Sisters," a classic wonder tale motif.

"Don Coyote and Don Conejo."   Submitted by Eduardo Sanchez, from his grandmother. An animal trickster tale from Ecuador that features a contest between two of the archetypal trickster characters, Rabbit and Coyote. The line between trickery and foolishness is a thin one, and in this case, Coyote crosses it first.

"Juan Bobo's Pig."   Miriam Veliz, a bilingual Spanish teacher from Puerto Rico, told me this story in the Roosevelt teachers' lounge. This is the best known of the cycle of "Juan Bobo" ("Foolish Juan") stories from Puerto Rico. See the Mexican and Philippine versions ("Juan El

Huevon" and "Lazy Juan"). This version was previously included in *More Ready-to-Tell Tales,* edited by David Holt and Bill Mooney.

Eastern Europe

"Chicken's Great Adventure."   Submitted by Adis Cesir, from his grandmother. A fine Bosnian version of a familiar formula or chain tale in which the search for a desired result leads to a series of linked and closely patterned episodes.

"Baka and Dika."   Submitted by Adis Cesir, from his grandmother. Another Bosnian formula tale.

"The Sickness of the Wolf."   Submitted by Aida Kaplanovic, from her father. An Eastern European animal trickster tale featuring the chief European trickster hero, Reynard, the Fox. The potential political overtones of this fable are hard to overlook in the context of recent Serbian-Muslim conflicts.

"The Youngest Son and the Queen of Beauty."   Submitted by Medisa Brkic, from her neighbor. A wonder tale featuring the motif of the youngest son and the animal bride, so beloved by psychoanalytically minded folklorists. There are endless parallels in Grimm (e.g., "The Three Feathers") and around the world.

"The Fairy's Clothes."   Submitted by Goran Jesic. The floating legend motif of the woman of the other world who can be captured by hiding her magic clothing is well-known in Celtic countries (there are hundreds of versions from Ireland and Scotland, including the famous seal or "silkie" stories). This is the first version I have seen from the Balkans. "Hassan and the Swan Woman of the Island of the Djinn" (see p. 139) shows how the same motif can be embedded in a traditional wonder tale.

"Nasruddin Hodja."   Submitted by Majda Mujkanovic, Edin Kadunic, Alen Potkrajac, Admir Rosic, and Amela Pojak. Nasrudin is the Jack of the Muslim world, a trickster/fool character whose lore is known all across the range of Islamic culture, from southern Spain to Palestine and from Persia to China. He is known by many names, including Nasruddin in Iran and Afghanistan, Hodja in Bosnia and Turkey, Gioha in Arabia and North Africa, Giufa in Sicily. Certain tales told on Nasruddin are also told about other folkloric trickster/fools, such as Jack, Coyote, Brer Rabbit, the Wise Men of Chelm, or Gopal the Jester. But many are unique to this culture and show a wry yet sophisticated approach to human psychology (see the collections of Sufi writer Idries Shah). According to Turkish sources, there was an actual thirteenth-century cleric by the name of Nasreddin Hodja, born in 1208 in Central Anatolia, who lived as a religious teacher in the town of Aksehir until his death in 1284. But the traditional stories attributed to his name are literally endless. If you tell a few of them to a class of students (or cab drivers!) from anywhere in the Islamic world you are bound to hear some new ones in return.

"Two Friends."   Submitted by Ardit Shero. Two short Albanian joke fables, similar in style to the Nasrudin tales.

"The Dark Place."   Submitted by Radovan Mitrovic, from a family friend. A strange and chilling fable from Serbia, full of overtones of the region's tragic history.

"The Grandmother's Eyes."   Submitted by Radovan Mitrovic, from his grandmother. An exceedingly dark wonder tale from Serbia, with echoes of the Old Testament Jacob wrestling with the angel.

"Grandmother March."   Submitted by George Popov, from his mother. A lovely allegory of the months of Spring, with literary and ritual overtones. According to George, "This Bulgarian tradition symbolizes the end of the winter and the coming of spring. On the first of March each year Bulgarians give each other *martenitsa*—small figures made of white and red threads. People put them on their clothes or wrists and wish each other health and happiness.

The colors of the *martenitsa* have a special place in the Bulgarian tradition and customs. Red is a symbol of longevity. That is the reason why the custom takes place at the end of the winter, when the vitality of the body has run out. According to the custom, one has to wear *martenitsa* until he or she sees a stork, a swallow, or a blossoming tree. Then the *martenitsa* is tied on a tree in order to have good health during the year." This story has parallels in longer eastern European wonder tales in which all the months of the year are personified.

"The Pity."   Submitted by Milena Deltcheva, from her father. A Bulgarian wisdom story, turning on a play on words that fortunately works well enough in translation.

"Fat Frumos and Ileana Consinzeana."   Submitted by Nicoleta Iordache, from her mother. A full and fine Romanian version of a classic wonder tale. The motif of fighting a dragon to win the hand of a princess is known the world over and practically defines the wonder tale hero.

"The Three Fawns."   Dorca Stirbu, from her mother. The standard Romanian version of "The Three Little Pigs."

"Rooster and Fox."   Submitted by Iryna Martyniv, from her mother and a family friend. An Aesopian animal trickster tale with a double reverse twist. Fables about the clever Fox are the chief animal trickster type in Western and Eastern Europe (see "The Sickness of the Wolf").

"The Golden Ring."   Submitted by Iryna Martyniv, from her mother and a family friend. A wonder tale featuring a youngest-best hero. Ivan is the Slavic form of Jack, and this is a typical adventure for Jack in his questing phase.

"One Eye, Two Eyes, and Three Eyes."   Submitted by Iryna Martyniv, from her mother and a family friend. One of the more common variants of the Cinderella tale type. In the Southern Appalachians this same tale is also woven around Jack (Chase, "Jack and the Bull Strap"). Iryna was an honor student at Mather who not only submitted three lovely stories to this book, she also brought in some fine examples of Ukrainian needlepoint design.

"No Accident."   A traditional religious legend from the Lubavitch Hasidim, an Orthodox Jewish sect dating to the early eighteenth century. The North Side of Chicago has a network of strongly traditional Jewish neighborhoods in which centuries-old modes of Torah study and ritual are strictly observed. The art teacher at Senn High School, Barbara Singer, who passed this and "Diamonds and Onions" to me, had spent considerable time with members of the Lubavitch, who were her neighbors in West Rogers Park. Another version of this story can be found in Howard Schwartz's collection, *Gabriel's Palace: Jewish Mystical Tales*.

"Diamonds and Onions."   A parable, a form of religious teaching widespread in Eastern European Jewish culture. A related tale, attributed to the famous eighteenth-century Jewish preacher known as the Dubner Maggid, can be found in Peninnah Schramm's *Stories within Stories: From the Jewish Oral Tradition*.

The Middle East

"The Inheritance."   Submitted by Amal Ali Mohammed, from her grandmother. A wisdom tale from Palestine, which has parallels in many sources, including Aesop. Amal, Nahil, and Iyab (who liked to be called David) Mohammed Abdel-Majid were siblings or half-siblings from a large Palestinian family at Roosevelt High School. They began telling me traditional stories from my first day in their classrooms. Their grandmother must have been a notable storyteller— "She told us a hundred stories," they would say, by way of meaning, "lots." She was gone by then, but the first four stories in this chapter are the ones they remembered best.

"Ajlooka."   Submitted by Amal Ali Mohammed, from her grandmother. An unusual find: a female folktale heroine who is both beautiful and foolish. This and the next story feature Ajlooka, my best transliteration of her Arabic name. In this one, she disobeys her mother and so winds up eaten by a desert ghoul, which my young informants called the *wahash*.

Traditional cultures are far more likely than ours to allow central characters in their stories to be killed, especially for the crime of disobedience.

"Ajlooka and the Gas Seller."   Submitted by Nahil Abdel-Majid, from her grandmother. The traditional foolish wife story (the best known version of which in this country is the one from Chase's *Grandfather Tales*) with an Arabic twist, the search for a name that would match her beauty. The last episode, the husband's flight and return when he finds three people more foolish than his wife, is also in the Appalachian version.

"The Grandfather's Plate."   Submitted by Iyab (David) Mohammed and Nahil Abdel-Majid. Another traditional wisdom tale, known in versions from Ireland to India.

"The Three Cows."   Submitted by Abdel Aly Habib, from his grandfather. A fable from the Aesopic tradition.

"Gioha Teaches the People to Pray."   Submitted by Suad Saeed, from her brother. Gioha (Nasruddin) at his subversive best.

"The Most Intelligent Donkey," "The Answer to Everything," and "Gratitude."   Three Syrian examples of Gioha's crazy wisdom. Mazen Bittar, who submitted these tales, wrote, "My Grandfather remembered hearing a lot of stories about Gioha. He used to sit with his friends around the fire at night, telling jokes and tales." Mazen was already quite a man of the world, supporting an extended family while finishing his last year of American high school.

"Hassan and the Swan Woman of the Island of the Djinn."   Submitted by Suad Saeed, from her father. A tale from Yemen that incorporates the hiding-of-the-fairy's-clothing motif from the well-known legend (see "The Fairy's Clothes") into a much longer wonder tale framework. The *djinn* are creatures of the Arabic Otherworld, like the Celtic *sidhe* or the Mexican *duendes*.

"Does Your Father Have Horns on his Head?"   Submitted by Suad Saeed, from her father. A fool tale from Yemen, with parallels in Ireland, Scotland, and Appalachia. The mother of this fool would know exactly what Jack's poor mother went through, though they lived a world apart.

"The Young Man Who Made a Fortune from a Grain of Corn."   Submitted by Yusra Mohammed, from her father. A Yemeni trickster tale, with a formulaic design familiar in European and Appalachian parallels.

"The Daughter Whose Stomach Got Big."   Submitted by Afrah Abdelquawi, from her grandmother. A frightening Yemeni version of the wicked-stepmother/abandoned step-daughter motif. The legendary element of the reptile in the belly that starves its host is found in folkloric beliefs worldwide. A particularly vivid version is in Douglas Hyde's *Beside the Fire*, collected in Ireland in the 1890s. There is also a version in the *Panchatantra*.

Africa

"The Lazy Donkey."   Submitted by Hana Koya. Two linked fables from the Aesopic tradition. The two episodes in this version could be each told as separate fables. The legendary Aesop was supposed to have been born in Ethiopia and sold into slavery in Greece in the sixth century B.C., which means that these fables may have remained in oral tradition in Aesop's homeland for at least 2,600 years.

"Hyena and Fox."   Submitted by Allai Andu. An Eritrean children's story that takes the familiar motifs of the three baby animals and the enemy with the disguised voice (see "The Three Fawns") and places it within a framework of horror and revenge.

"The Three Servants."   Submitted by Aster Eshetu. The motif of the worthy and unworthy servants in this Ethipian tale is closely related to the youngest-best daughter motif, found in folktales the world over, the best-known version being "Cinderella."

"Alaqa Giibri-Hanna."   Submitted by Mehret Maru. This is an Ethiopian trickster/fool folktale hero in the mold of Nasrudin. Like Nasruddin, the stories are based on the exploits and witticisms of an actual historical figure. According to a 1955 article from the *Journal of American Folklore*, Alaqa (Chief) Giibri-Hanna was a provincial scholar from the Gondar region of Ethiopia at the end of the nineteenth century who was well-known around the country for his repartee and his scandalous life. Stories about him are still widely circulated today.

"Egal Shidaad."   Submitted by Rahama Hassan, from her older sister. Another trickster/fool folktale hero, this character has a peculiar twist: cowardice. Known as "the Wise Coward Man" (Hassan), Egal Shidaad's wily ways of avoiding danger are much loved among the no-madic people of Somalia.

"The Dancing Tree."   Submitted by Adebayo Charles Isijola. The principle trickster character in the folktales of the Yoruba people of Nigeria is Tortoise. In the Nigerian Tortoise cycle, the animal we know today only gradually takes shape, as each of his misadventures brings about another corrective change in his form and nature. This one features an original African version of the "tar baby" motif, which in this case is the device of a fetish-priest or witch doctor. Thus it shows the African religious roots of the most famous Brer Rabbit tale from Joel Chandler Harris' "Uncle Remus" collections.

"Yams for the Taking."   Submitted by Adebayo Charles Isijola. See note to "The Dancing Tree," above.

"How Tortoise Broke His Shell."   Submitted by Anthony Lawal. Also known as "Tortoise and the Birds," probably the best-known Nigerian folktale.

"Why Tortoise's Head Is Bald."   Submitted by Anthony Lawal. Yet another Tortoise tale with an explanatory twist. For an additional adventure of this Yoruba trickster hero, see "Hot Pepper and Boiling Water" in Chapter 2.

"The Dwarf Baby."   Submitted by Edward Boateng. A supernatural legend. The *abwateia* is an African member of the elf family, and this story from the Twi tribe of Ghana is related to many tales of changelings and fairy kidnappings from the British Isles and elsewhere. It also features a triumphantly lazy younger son who bears a striking resemblance to Jack.

"The Magic Cane."   Submitted by Edward Boateng. A cautionary fable about the handling of power. In the animistic worldview of traditional African religion this type of story can be adapted to portray literal beliefs or metaphorical lessons.

"The Two Brothers."   Submitted by Aisha Aboagye. Versions of this musical folktale about a singing bone that informs on its murderer are found from India to Scandinavia. European and American versions usually feature two sisters, and the bone is often made into a fiddle or a harp. The crime-and-punishment motif in the story also echoes the tale called "The Juniper Tree" in Grimm, and the biblical tale of Cain and Abel.

"Anansi the Spider."   Submitted by Aisha Aboagye. Anansi is the signature trickster of the Ashanti people of West Africa. Many from this tribe were taken into slavery to the Carribean and the plantations of coastal South Carolina and Georgia, and so Anansi stories have taken root there, too, especially in Jamaica, where the storytellers changed Anansi's gender and called him "Aunt Nancy."

Asia

"The Four Wishes."   Submitted by Jason Galang. A fine Philippine version of "The Fisherman and his Wife" (Grimm). Alexander Pushkin wrote a Russian version in verse, "The Golden Fish," that became one of the best-known stories of that culture—several of my Russian students at Mather turned in tales based on it. A popular English version is "The Old Woman Who Lived in a Vinegar Bottle" (MacDonald). The fisherman's name in Jason Galang's version links him with the Foolish Juan, Juan Bobo, and Jack tale traditions.

"Lazy Juan." Submitted by January Valdez. A typical Foolish Juan story about a boy who can't follow instructions. See "Juan Bobo's Pig" for a Puerto Rican entry in the worldwide series. The most popular Anglo-American type is "Jack's First Job" (Holt and Mooney, 42)

"The Enchanted Adarna Bird." Submitted by January Valdez. A wonder tale with a youngest-best son for its hero, making it a member of the worldwide Jack tale extended family. The motif of the magical bird is found in Grimm ("The Golden Bird") and in Russian collections ("The Firebird").

"The Wise Rabbit and the Forest Sprite." Submitted by Reath Lim, from his father. The motif of putting the genie into a bottle is well known in Indian and Arabic folktales. The mischievous tree spirit is characteristic of the animist traditions of East Asia, while the trickster rabbit connects the story in an interesting way to African and African-American traditions.

"Why Cat and Tiger Are No Longer Friends." Submitted by Hanh Pham, from a friend. An animal fable that is found in Aesop's fables.

"Brotherhood." Submitted by Thai Ly, from his father. Vietnamese have a special fondness for stories about family love, as this story and the next three demonstrate. Curiously though, this same story is told in the Jewish commentaries on the Old Testament, the Talmud, to explain why God picked the original site for the building of the Temple in Jerusalem.

"Areca Nut, Betel Plant, and Limestone." Submitted by Hanh Pham and Luu Nguyen, from their mothers. Another story about brotherly love, which also provides a legendary explanation for the origin of two popular herbal stimulants in Southeast Asian culture.

"The Bunch of Chopsticks." Submitted by Nha Huynh and Luu Nguyen, from their mothers. A fable of family unity, told around the world, including in Aesop's fables.

"The Ghost Pig." Submitted by Thai Ly. A first-person account of a supernatural visitor. The traditional aspect is in the beliefs it embodies in the survival of family love after death, even among these most characteristically Asian of food-providing animals.

"Gopal the Jester." Submitted by Ajay Patel, from his uncle. Gopal Bhand is a legendary trickster fool in Bengali culture. Gopal is supposed to have been a real person, like Nasruddin or Alaqa Giibri-Hanna. According to Bengali legend, he was a barber and jester at the court of Raja Krishnachandra Roy in the eighteenth century. Like the stories of Birbal (see below), Gopal stories exemplify the way comic folktales accumulate around certain key cultural figures. Knowing the names of these figures can be like a passport to the storytelling worlds of their cultural children. Gopal and Birbal are both popular figures in contemporary Indian comics and picture books.

"The Lamp on the Tower." Submitted by Sumaiya Patel. A Birbal tale with parallels in the Nasruddin cycle (see "The Sound of the Coins"). There is also a well-known version from Ethiopia, the title story of Harold Courlander and Wolf Leslau's *Fire On the Mountain* (1950; reprinted in Joanna Cole's collection *Best Loved Folktales of the World*). Birbal was a minister in the court of the Moghul Emperor Akbar (1556–1605).

"The Hand of God." Submitted by Sumaiya Patel. Another wisdom tale with the same form as the previous tales of Gopal and Birbal, that is, a royal advisor whose wisdom or cleverness is initially the cause for punishment, then vindication. The respect for learning that is so widespread in Indian culture is strongly reinforced by this genre of tale.

"The Dutti Malen." Submitted by Sumaiya Patel. A tale in the popular romance genre—a tragedy based on consequences of the caste system and the incest taboo. It is also what folklorists call a *cante fable*, or song-story, with its repeating verse that Sumaiya Patel sang to a beautifully elaborate Indian melody. Sumaiya (who also submitted "The Lamp on the Tower" and "The Hand of God") said that when she was nine or ten years old back in India, she and friends would sit in a circle on the playground at recess and tell each other these stories.

"The Surprised Thief."   Submitted by Ajay Patel, from his father. A trickster/fool tale that is told in Muslim communities, featuring Nasruddin. The Sufi writer Idries Shah says that this kind of story is often used in teaching situations to show the power of the unconscious personality.

"The Monkey's Heart."   Submitted by Sajimon Thekkumkattil and Joshy Puthethu, from Sajimon's uncle. Also collected in Gujerati by Shailesh and Nayan Patel. A tale from the *Panchatantra*, a collection of fables from Kashmir, which, at over 2,200 years old, is one of the oldest collections of stories in the world.

"The Good-hearted Daughter."   Submitted by Saiyada Maria, from her father. Another version of the good and wicked step-daughters motif (for a Guatemalan version, see "The Fairy Falin").

"The Strongest of All Creatures."   Submitted by Saiyada Maria, from her father. A circular wisdom tale, popular in Asia, and very expressive of the Buddhist and Hindu cyclical view of life and of the self. Compare with the Japanese story of "The Stonecutter" (McDermott). Saiyada, a Roosevelt student, turned in a collection of 334 Urdu proverbs, along with two excellent folktales.

"Planting Gold."   Submitted by Mohsin Mirza, from his mother who heard it from her grandmother. A Nasruddin tale from Pakistan. Like many stories in this cycle, it turns on the human penchant for self-deception.

"The Milkman and the Monkeys."   Submitted by Mohsin Mirza. Another tale about honesty and deceit. Here the monkeys take the trickster role of articulate conscience that in the previous story is played by Nasruddin.

"The Sparrow and His Friends."   Submitted by Hina Salam. A story that places the concepts of truth and deception in a very different light. This fable is retold in the works of the thirteenth-century Persian Sufi poet and teacher Jalaluddin Rumi to bring home the lesson that spiritual knowledge must often be transmitted indirectly (Shah, *Tales of the Dervishes* 189).

"The Honest Woodsman."   Submitted by Sumara Khalid, from her sister-in-law. A fable, also found in Aesop, in which the conscience-testing role is played by an angel (or perhaps a djinn, a member of a race of supernatural beings widespread in Eastern folklore). In Aesop, the part is played by the god Mercury.

"Patience."   Submitted by Sumara Khalid, from her sister-in-law. A delightful Pakistani wonder tale featuring the motif of an enchanted bridegroom redeemed by love—similar in essence to "Beauty and the Beast" and "East of the Sun, West of the Moon," though formally more compact. This version presents the ancient motif attired in a beautifully fitted and embroidered garment of traditional Muslim culture.

INDEX OF STORIES BY TITLE

INDEX OF STORIES BY LANGUAGE AND COUNTRY OF ORIGIN

ABOUT THE AUTHOR

Storyteller, musician, composer, folklorist, and author, Joseph Sobol is an artist of wide-ranging accomplishments. A resident artist in North Carolina's prestigious Visiting Artist Program from 1985–1989, he received a doctorate in performance studies from Northwestern University in 1994 and toured the country from 1994–1999 with his award-winning musical theater piece, "In the Deep Heart's Core," based on the works of Irish poet W. B. Yeats. Joseph has released a cassette and four CDs of music and stories, alone and with his group Kiltartan Road. His book *The Storytellers' Journey: An American Revival,* published in 1999, tells the story of the women and men of the contemporary storytelling renaissance in the United States. With the support of the Chicago Department of Cultural Affairs he created the Chicago TESOL Folklore Project to teach folklore and storytelling to immigrant children in secondary TESOL classes. Since 2000 he has directed the Graduate Program in Storytelling at East Tennessee State University.